LEADING
— IN —
TOUGH
TIMES

Also by John Maxwell

LEADING
— IN —
TOUGH
TIMES

**OVERCOME EVEN THE GREATEST
CHALLENGES WITH COURAGE
AND CONFIDENCE**

JOHN C. MAXWELL

CENTER
STREET

NEW YORK   NASHVILLE

The author is represented by Yates & Yates, LLP, Literary Agency, Santa Ana, California.

Center Street
Hachette Book Group
1290 Avenue of the Americas, New York, NY 10104
centerstreet.com
twitter.com/centerstreet

First Edition: July 2021

Center Street is a division of Hachette Book Group, Inc. The Center Street name and logo are trademarks of Hachette Book Group, Inc.

The publisher is not responsible for websites (or their content) that are not owned by the publisher.

The Hachette Speakers Bureau provides a wide range of authors for speaking events. To find out more, go to www.HachetteSpeakersBureau.com or call (866) 376-6591.

Names: Maxwell, John C., 1947—author.
Title: Leading in tough times : overcome even the greatest challenges with courage and confidence / John C. Maxwell.
Identifiers: LCCN 2021006599 | ISBN 9781546029380 (hardcover) | ISBN 9781546029373 (ebook)
Subjects: LCSH: Executive ability. | Leadership. | Teams in the workplace—Psychological aspects. | Communication in management. | Crisis management.
Classification: LCC HD38.2 .M3922 2021 | DDC 658.4/092—dc23
LC record available at https://lccn.loc.gov/2021006599

ISBNs: 978-1-5460-2938-0 (hardcover), 978-1-5460-2937-3 (ebook)

Printed in the United States of America

LSC-C

Printing 1, 2021

Contents

I want to say thank you to Charlie Wetzel and the rest of the team who assisted me with the formation and publication of this book. And to the people in my organizations who support it: You all add incredible value to me, which allows me to add value to others. Together, we're making a difference!

Tough Times

Invitation to Opportunity

As human beings, we seem to believe that life is supposed to be easy. This is particularly a problem in America today. We expect a smooth and easy road to success. We expect our lives to be hassle-free. We expect the government to solve our problems. We expect to get the prize without having to pay the price. That is not reality! Life is hard.

In *Life's Greatest Lessons*, Hal Urban writes,

Once we accept the fact that life is hard, we begin to grow. We begin to understand that every problem is also an opportunity. It is then that we dig down and discover what we're made of. We begin to accept the challenges of life. Instead of letting our hardships defeat us, we welcome them as a test of character. We use them as a means of rising to the occasion.[1]

This reality is especially important for leaders to recognize and embrace. Nothing worth having in life comes without effort. That is why psychiatrist M. Scott Peck begins his book *The Road Less Traveled* with the words "Life is difficult." If we don't understand and accept the truth that life is difficult, that leadership is difficult, then we set ourselves up for failure and we won't learn or succeed.

As leaders, even if we are willing to concede that life is difficult for most people, deep down inside many of us secretly hope somehow that this truth won't apply to us. But no one escapes life's problems, failures, and challenges. If we are to make progress, we must do so through life's difficulties. Or as poet Ralph Waldo Emerson stated it, "The walking of Man is falling forwards."

The Advantages of Adversity

Good leaders understand that adversity and challenges are actually opportunities to rise up in leadership.

1. Adversity Introduces Us to Ourselves

Adversity always gets our attention. We can't ignore it. It causes us to stop and look at our situation. And at ourselves if we have the courage. Adversity creates an opportunity for self-discovery. As the great Egyptian leader Anwar el-Sadat said, "Great suffering builds up a human being and puts him within the reach of self-knowledge." This I believe is true—if we embrace it.

One of my favorite books is *As a Man Thinketh* by James Allen. My father required me to read it when I was in my early teens. One of the ideas that left the strongest impression on me as a youth was this: "Circumstance does not make the man; it reveals him to himself."

2. Adversity Is a Better Teacher Than Success

Adversity comes to us as a teaching tool. You've probably heard the saying "When the pupil is ready, the teacher will come." That is not necessarily true. With adversity, the teacher will come whether the pupil is ready or not. Those who are ready learn from the teacher. Those who are not don't learn. Oprah Winfrey advises, "Turn your wounds into wisdom." Leaders can do that only when they have the right mind-set.

3. Adversity Opens Doors for New Opportunities

One of the greatest lessons I've learned as a leader is that adversity is often the door to opportunity. Good entrepreneurs know this instinctively, but most people have been trained to see adversity the wrong way. As speaker and cofounder of the Rich Dad Company, Kim Kiyosaki, observed, "Most of us are taught, beginning in kindergarten, that mistakes are bad. How often did you hear, 'Don't make a mistake!' In reality, the way we learn is by *making* mistakes. A mistake simply shows you something you didn't know. Once you make the mistake, then you know it. Think about the first time you touched a hot stove (the mistake). From making that mistake, you learned that if you touch a hot stove you get burned. A mistake isn't bad; it's there to teach you something."

When many people face adversity, they let it get them down. Instead, they need to look for the benefit or opportunity. One of my favorite examples of this occurred with Procter & Gamble back in the 1870s. One day at the factory, an employee went to lunch and forgot to turn off the machinery that was mixing the soap. When he returned, the soap had increased in volume because air had been whipped into it. What a mistake!

What should he do? He didn't want to throw it out, so he poured it into the frames, and it was cut, packaged, and shipped, even though he had ruined it.

A few weeks later, the company began receiving letters from customers asking for more orders of the soap that floated. Why? The soap was used in factories. At the end of their shift, factory workers washed at vats of standing water that became murky. Bars of soap that floated were easier to find when dropped. A manufacturing mistake led to an opportunity, the creation of Ivory soap, which is still sold today, more than one hundred years later.

As you face tough times, are you seeing the opportunities? Are you looking for ways to take advantage of them?

4. Adversity Writes Our Story If Our Response Is Right

Some leaders treat adversity as a stepping-stone, others as a tombstone. The difference in the way they approach it depends on how they see it. Performance psychologist Jim Loehr says, "Champions have taught us how to take an experience and essentially write the story of its effect. If you see a failure as an opportunity to learn and get better, it will be. If you perceive it as a mortal blow, it will be. In that way, the power of the story is more important than the experience itself."

If you respond right to adversity, you see it as something that can help you to become better than you were before. I read a poem years ago by James Casey called "Climb the Steep." The first stanza says,

> For every hill I've had to climb
> For every rock that bruised my feet
> For all the blood and sweat and grime
> For blinding storms and burning heat
> My heart sings but a grateful song
> These were the things that made me strong[2]

What kind of story will tough times write in your life? Every leader gets a chance to be the hero in a potentially great story. Some step up to that role and some don't. The choice is yours.

Good leaders see and seize opportunities. They are continually on the lookout for ways to help their organizations and advance their teams. Leadership authors James M. Kouzes and Barry Z. Posner liken leaders to the settlers who founded the United States or tamed the western frontier. They write, "Leaders are pioneers—people who are willing to step out into the unknown. They are people who are willing to take risks, to innovate and experiment in order to find new and better ways of doing things."

Leaders, by definition, are out front. They take new territory and others follow them. Great leaders don't merely send others out in times of trouble. They lead the charge. They're more like tour guides than travel agents. They see opportunities, prepare to move forward, and then say, "Follow me."

Lead People Through Sustained Difficult Times

One of the most challenging tasks any leader faces is being a change agent and leading people through tough times. But it can also be one of the most rewarding. Economist John Kenneth Galbraith asserted, "All of the great leaders have had one characteristic in common: it was the willingness to confront unequivocally the major anxiety of their people in their time."

In tough times the people we lead find out who we are, and we also find out what we're made of. As author Jack Kinder says, "You're not made in a crisis—you're revealed. When you squeeze an orange—you get orange juice. When you squeeze a lemon—you get lemon juice. When a human being gets squeezed—you get what is inside—positive or negative."

The best way to approach tough times is to try to see them as opportunities. Most people want their problems to be fixed without their having to face them, but that is an impossibility. As a leader, as a coach, as a catalyst for turnaround, you need to help people solve problems, take responsibility, and work to make things better. They need help, which you can give them in the form of advice, encouragement, and positive reinforcement, but everyone needs to do his or her part and work together.

With that context in mind, here is how I would recommend that you lead and serve people during difficult times:

1. Define Reality

Management expert Peter Drucker said, "A time of turbulence is a dangerous time, but its greatest danger is a temptation to deny reality." So what is a leader to do? Define reality for people. That is a leader's first responsibility.

The Law of the Scoreboard in my book *The 17 Indisputable Laws of Teamwork* says the team can make adjustments when it knows where it stands. As the leader of a team, you need to help people define the things that are holding them back. Then you need to define the things that will free them up. People cannot make good choices if they don't know what these things are, and many have a hard time figuring them out on their own. You're there to help them. And as *Roots* author Alex Haley observed, "Either you deal with what is the reality, or you can be sure that the reality is going to deal with you."

2. Remind Them of the Big Picture

Leaders are keepers and communicators of the vision. They bear the responsibility for always seeing the big picture and helping their people to see it. People need to be reminded of why they are doing what they do, and of the benefits that await them as a reward for their hard work. That doesn't mean that the vision is 100 percent clear to the leader, especially during difficult times. But that's okay. When I'm leading people through a difficult situation, I often don't know all the answers. But I know there are answers, and I will do everything I can to make sure we find out what they are. That gives people reassurance.

3. Help Them Develop a Plan

Before you can develop a strategy to get out of a difficult situation, you must know where you are and where you want to go. If you have helped people by defining reality and showing them the big picture, the next task is to identify the steps required to go from here to there.

Not everyone finds it easy to do that. As a leader, you need to come alongside them and help them figure it out.

4. Help Them Make Good Choices

People's choices define who they are and determine where they go. It's true that we don't choose everything we get in life, but much of what we get comes from what we've chosen. For you as a leader, the more good choices you have made throughout your life, the better you have probably positioned yourself to help others, not only because you have gained experience and developed wisdom, but also because repeated good choices often lead to personal success and greater options. If these things are true for you, put them to good use by helping others navigate difficult waters.

5. Value and Promote Teamwork

When times get tough, everybody needs to work together if they want to get the team out of trouble. The Law of Mount Everest in *The 17 Indisputable Laws of Teamwork* states, "As the challenge escalates, the need for teamwork elevates." No team can win and keep winning unless everyone works together. It's the responsibility of leaders to promote teamwork and get team members cooperating and working together.

6. Give Them Hope

John W. Gardner, former secretary of health, education, and welfare, said, "The first and last task of a leader is to keep hope alive—the hope that we can finally find our way through to a better world—despite the day's action, despite our own inertness and shallowness and wavering resolve." Hope is the foundation of change. If we continue to hold hope high, and we help others to do the same, there is always a chance to move forward and succeed.

Productive organizations led by strong leaders are hard to beat. Their effectiveness is high, and so is their morale. Former general George C. Marshall said, "Morale is the state of mind. It is steadfastness and courage and hope. It is confidence and zeal and loyalty.... It is staying power, the spirit which endures to the end—the will to win. With it all things are possible, without it everything else ... is for naught."

✳   ✳   ✳

Crisis holds the opportunity to be reborn. Difficult times can discipline us to become stronger. Conflict can actually renew our chances of building better relationships.

It's not always easy to remember these things. As leaders, our job is to remind people of the possibilities and to help them succeed.

Many people in leadership positions try to solve problems by using systems. Or they pay others to try to solve problems for them. But the truth is, leaders cannot delegate the solving of problems to someone else. They have to be active in facing challenges, breaking through obstacles, putting out fires, correcting mistakes, and directing people. And once their effectiveness becomes contagious and spreads throughout the team, productivity begins to solve many problems—many more than management or consultants ever will.

1

The Self-Leadership Challenge

Preparing Yourself for the Journey

The first step you must take as you approach tough times is to prepare yourself as a leader. You need to make yourself ready for the challenge of leading others through adversity. Of course, you must lead yourself well and make good choices. But you should also think about what kind of leader you want to be as you lead your team forward. Knowing yourself as a leader, what works best and is most effective for you and your team, is important at any time. But when you face new challenges or significant change that impacts the work environment and your goals, you need to really think through who you are going to be to your team and make sure that you remain true to your values, no matter how difficult the journey gets or how much pressure you will be under.

You Are Here

Faced with tough times, leaders instinctively start searching for a way forward. But they don't always pay enough attention to their starting point. The first step of self-leadership is self-evaluation. You can't get where you want to go until you know where you are. By answering the following questions, you'll be better equipped to map your journey through the tough times you face.

Know Yourself

Successful leaders work hard at self-awareness. They know their own strengths and weaknesses. They examine and understand their temperament. They know what personal experiences have served them well. They know their energy level, their daily, monthly, and seasonal rhythms. They know which kinds of people they work well with and which kinds they have to try harder to appreciate. They have a sense of where they want to go and how they can get there. As a result, they know what they're capable of doing, and their leadership is steady.

Knowing yourself on a pretty deep level isn't quick or easy. It is a long and involved process. Some of it isn't particularly fun. But it is necessary if you want to become a better leader. Self-knowledge is foundational to effective leading.

Determine What You Stand for and Value

This is the heart of your character and your leadership. Values are the criteria you use to drive your behavior. We all must decide what values we will embrace—i.e., what we will live for, what we would die for. And if you're a leader, those values that you embrace—and model—will also determine who follows you and why.

If you haven't given much dedicated thought to what your values are, begin by writing down any and every principle or thing that is important to you. List every admirable character quality you can think of. As an aspect of your life comes to mind, try to capture what's important to you about it. Ultimately, your values should not be determined by externals, such as your profession or your environment, but it's a good idea to consider such things in order to be thorough in your thinking.

When you think you've exhausted every possible idea, set the list aside for a while but keep thinking about it in the back of your mind. When new ideas come, add them to the list. You may also want to do some reading to stir your thinking and see if you've missed anything.

After a few weeks, begin to combine ideas on the list. (For example, "truthfulness" and "integrity" really overlap. So do "commitment" and "hard work." Choose one—or pick another word that better describes both terms together.) Then narrow the list down. You can't possibly keep track of how well you live out twenty or fifty values. Start by eliminating anything that's superficial or temporary. Then identify which values are based on truth and your highest ideals. Which items on your list truly represent the core of your being? Which will be lasting? What would you be willing to live for? To die for?

While your values remain the same in both your personal and professional life, here are some specific values that I believe are crucial when it comes to leadership:

Servanthood: Leading Well Means Serving Others

People pursue leadership for many reasons. Some want power. Others seek riches. Many are driven by an ideology or a desire to change the world. I believe the only worthy motivation for leadership is a desire to serve. If you want to lead but are unwilling to serve people, I think you need to check your motives. Leaders who do not put people first will ultimately disqualify themselves as leaders, because their people will lose trust in them. If you are willing to embrace servant-hood, not only will you become a better leader, you will help your team, help the people your team serves, and make the world a better place.

Purpose: Let Your Why Direct Your What

You can't grow to your potential if you don't know your purpose. And if you don't know why you're on this earth and you are not able to improve in that purpose to the best of your ability, you'll be very limited in the ways you can help others. Once you understand your purpose, you need to prioritize your life according to that purpose. If you don't, you'll continually get off track and you may never feel a real sense of fulfillment and completion.

Integrity: Live the Life Before You Lead Others

Great teams are made up of people with diverse skills. But when it comes to values, habits, disciplines, and attitudes, there needs to be unity. That starts with the example set by the leader. If the leader is undisci-plined, does sloppy work, wastes time, or treats people poorly, the people will follow suit. If you do more than you expect of others, others will respect you, and the chances are good that they will be willing to follow you.

Relationships: Walk Slowly Through the Crowd

A lot of leaders assume that people will come to them if they need or want something. But good leaders don't think that way. Effective leaders initiate. They communicate vision. They seek out opportunities. They start initiatives that will benefit the organization. And they initiate with people too. They want good relationships with the people who work with them, so they seek those people out. They ask them questions. They learn who they are. They offer assistance. They find ways for them to succeed. If you want to become a better leader, become highly relational.

Rededicate Yourself to Growth and Self-Discipline

Leaders need to keep growing in order to keep leading. They cannot expect their followers to grow and improve if they aren't doing so as well. This is especially important during tough times, because tough times bring change. And the only way to adapt to changes is to grow. Whether you're already pursuing growth or just recognizing your need for it, make a new commitment to making the changes to your behavior that are necessary to become the leader your people and the circumstances need. Tough times demand that you ...

Consistently Live Out Your Values

Hopefully, you've narrowed down the list of the values that you intend to stand for. But knowledge and intention aren't enough. You have to live out your values every day. Start by expanding your values list by writing next to each value a descriptive statement. It should explain how you intend to apply the value to your life, as well as the benefit or direction that it will bring. Keep that document where you can see it every day. Then establish the following daily habits. Work on them until you are consistent.

1. Embrace Your Values Daily

Remind yourself of your top values at the beginning of every day. Then, as you face decisions throughout the day, make choices that honor those values. During and after the decision, tell yourself—and others, when appropriate—*why* you made the choice that you did. It not only cements your values in your mind and helps you to practice them, but also adds a level of accountability.

2. Compare Your Values to Your Actions
   Constantly

Discord between values and actions creates chaos in a person's life. If you talk your values but neglect to walk them, then you will continually undermine your integrity and credibility. Take the time to compare every action you take with your values. Make note of when they matched or didn't match. For any behavior that didn't align with your values, you may need to revisit your decision to take that action. This information will help you make better decisions in the future. Resolve to make things right tomorrow, as needed. This will not feel easy, which leads to...

3. Live Out Your Values Regardless of Your
   Feelings

When you're feeling good and everything's going your way, it's not that difficult to consistently live out your values. However, when your values show that you need to take a stand or do something that will hurt or cost you, feelings like fear or anger can make it harder to follow through. To fight the temptation to do something based on feelings, click Pause. Feelings tend to decrease in intensity over time, allowing you to think more clearly. Resolve to prioritize your values over your feelings in every decision. Then practice this until your actions match what you say is most important. The goal is to do what's right no matter how you feel about it. Effective leaders make the hard decision and hope their feelings follow suit.

4. Evaluate Each Day in Light of Your Values

Most people take very little time to do any reflective thinking, yet that is necessary for anyone who wants to live out his values with consistency. Ben Franklin used to get up in the morning asking himself, "What good will I do today?" When he went to bed, he asked himself, "What good did I do today?" He was evaluating himself in light of one of his values.

Focus on Your Responsibilities, Not Your Rights

Just because you have the right to do something as a leader doesn't mean that it is the right thing to do. Changing your focus from rights to responsibilities is often a sign of maturity in a leader. Many of us are excited in early leadership years by the authority we have and what we can do with it. That power can be exhilarating, if not downright intoxicating. But each of us must strive to grow up and grow into a leadership role without relying on our rights. If we can mature in that way, we will start to change our focus from enjoying authority for its own sake to using authority to serve others.

Inevitably, leaders who focus on their rights develop a sense of entitlement. They expect their people to serve them, rather than looking for ways to serve their people. Their job description becomes more important to them than job development. They value protecting territory over promoting teamwork. As a result, values fall by the wayside and power becomes preeminent.

Leaders who pursue power emphasize rules and regulations that are to their advantage and ignore those that aren't. They also value relationships based only on the benefit to them. Their position in the hierarchy is the only thing that matters. But people who rely on their positions and titles are the weakest of all leaders. They expect their position to do the hard work for them in leadership, and they demand their rights. They give nothing. As a result, their people give their least and only follow them as far as they are required to. The team is not invested because their leader is not invested in them. They lack the motivation and inspiration to do their best work, and therefore the capacity of the team to produce results is limited.

Increase Your Leadership Courage

Let's face it: It can be difficult and risky to lead effectively, particularly when times are tough. Courage is necessary. With courage, leaders can take risks and go first when they need to. It helps them tackle big problems and face the possibility of failure.

Insecure leaders continually sabotage themselves and others. They worry about their position and standing. They are reluctant to take necessary risks. They have a hard time investing in other people because they fear that someone will take their place. For that reason, leaders who don't deal with their insecurities and develop courage rarely reach their full leadership potential.

If you suspect that your insecurities may be holding you back, then be prepared to do some work in the following areas:

Ego

Leaders who are honest with themselves know that they don't have all the answers. They recognize that success always comes from the combined contributions of everyone on a team. They don't try to answer every question themselves. They don't try to make every decision. They see winning as a collaborative effort. And their goal isn't to make others think more highly of them, it's to get their people to think more highly of themselves.

How can you tell if your ego might be getting in

the way of your ability to lead? Consider what happens when you meet with your team.

- Do your team members share their thoughts and ideas freely?
- Are the best ideas rarely your ideas?
- If you often contribute ideas, does the discussion quickly move from your idea to the best idea—and you're happy about it?

How about when your team performs?

- When your team succeeds, do the other team members get the majority of the credit?
- Is there a shared sense of pride in the work that's being done?
- When things go wrong, do you personally accept the greatest share of the blame?

If you can honestly answer yes to these questions, ego may not be a problem. If you answered no to many of those questions, beware. You may need to deal with your ego. Positive working environments led by secure leaders allow team members to get the credit. Confident leaders experience genuine joy in the success of others. When others shine, so do they.

Control

Many insecure workers try to avoid making mistakes by doing as little as possible or by trying to keep a low profile. Insecure leaders often deal with the issue differently. They rely on control. They think if they micromanage their people, they can keep them from making mistakes.

Unfortunately, controlling leaders don't understand that progress comes only from taking risks and making mistakes. Confident leaders forge ahead, break ground, and make mistakes. And they expect the same from their people.

Since you can't prevent mistakes, why not adopt an attitude in which you and your team learn from them? That's the only way anyone can really profit from mistakes anyway. Don't try to put people in a box. Try to help them make the most of their fumbles, flops, and failures. As Jack Welch, the former CEO of General Electric, said, "A leader's role is not to control people or stay on top of things, but rather to guide, energize, and excite." That's what confident leaders do.

Trust

Different leaders see trust in different ways. Secure leaders see it as the glue that keeps relationships together and makes business work. Insecure leaders don't place their trust in others, nor do they invest in others. As a result, they don't earn trust from others. As a leader, you should never take trust for granted. By increasing your courage, you will be able to give trust and earn it in return.

Seek Wisdom and Wins

Not everyone can develop leadership courage on their own. This is particularly true for young leaders with limited experience or guidance. Wise mentors and wins can affirm your decisions and increase your courage:

1. Spend Time with People Who Increase Your Courage

Many times we lack courage because the people we spend the most time with would rather take us down a notch than lift us up. If people in your life make you feel discouraged and tentative, you need to spend less time with them and more time with people who want to see you win and will encourage you to do courageous things.

2. Find Ways to Get a Few Wins Under Your Belt

If your courage isn't what it needs to be, find ways to rack up a few small victories. Success breeds confidence, no matter how small. Making a list of past victories can also help you develop (or regain) confidence. Remembering the positive results of courageous decisions will make the next decisions a little bit easier.

3. Quit Comparing Yourself to Others

Comparison weakens courage rather than strengthening it. In today's world, comparison is harder to avoid. Social media, for example, can compel you to compare your worst to others' best. In those situations, you will always find yourself lacking. Don't do it! Others are often not as good as we give them credit for, and we are all too aware of our weaknesses. As a result, the comparison is distorted. Besides, each of us is a unique individual with something to contribute to this world. Instead of comparing yourself to others, focus on being your best you.

4. Specialize Until You're Special

That leads to the final thing I would suggest you do to gain confidence. Become really great at something. If you specialize in doing something based on one of your top strengths, you not only add value to your team, you also find it easier to believe in yourself. If you want to gain confidence, become an expert in something. Develop a valuable skill. Learn everything there is to

know about your customers. It can be nearly anything—
if it helps the team to succeed and it gives you confidence, it's a win for everybody.

Courage sets individuals apart. Courageous people
stand out from the crowd. Courageous leaders offer certainty to uncertain people and security to insecure people, which is particularly important in troubled times.
People want to follow others who know where they're
going. A leader's courage is contagious for followers.
Together they are more likely to overcome adversity.

✴   ✴   ✴

Successful people who work well with others and who
relish challenges as well as opportunities don't see self-
leadership as negative or restrictive. They welcome it.
Vince Lombardi, legendary coach of the NFL's Green
Bay Packers, asserted, "I've never known a man worth
his salt who in the long run, deep down in his heart,
didn't appreciate the grind, the discipline." It's not easy
to stay true to your values and maintain a consistent
and beneficial leadership style when facing challenging
times. It takes self-leadership. But the rewards can be
remarkable.

2

The Change Challenge

Becoming an Effective Change Agent

How do people overcome problems, challenges, and difficulties? They make changes. Improvement requires change. Innovation requires change. Seizing opportunities requires change. However, at the same time, most human beings resist change.

That's why teams need good leaders—especially in tough times. Effective leaders make things happen. They get results. Not only are they productive individually, but they also are able to help their team to be successful. They find ways for the team and organization to win.

As a leader in tough times, you need to become a change agent. You need to help others embrace positive change, even when it takes them outside their comfort zone. You need to help them get results, even when they worry that it might not be possible.

Expect and Welcome Change

Leaders who succeed in leading their people through change have a unique perspective on the process. They expect, prepare for, and welcome it. Many people hope for change to happen, but few people want to actually change. Many leaders try to take their people through tough times without making changes. But effective leaders accept that it's necessary. More than that, they see it as a positive opportunity, and commit to find a way to lead their people through it.

I think many people see commitment as an event, something that is done in a moment. They say *I do* in a wedding ceremony. They shake hands to close a business deal. They buy a treadmill in order to exercise. But the commitment doesn't end with that decision; it's just getting started. And you better believe that anytime you make a commitment to something, it will be tested. Commitment is a process.

Commit to Being a Change Agent

There's a big difference between those who lead a successful change and critics who simply theorize about it. It's important to accept that change will be necessary. But knowledge is not enough. Leaders who are effective change agents manage to make change happen—regardless of how many obstacles they face, what the economy does, what kinds of problems their people experience, and so on. They fight for positive change because they know what's at stake!

Committed change agents keep their team moving forward. If they gain momentum, they don't back off and coast. They press on and increase that momentum so they can make bigger changes. And they help their people do the same. The process of leading change requires the change agent to...

Find Common Ground

The best way to start working as a change agent is the same as when trying to build a relationship. You need to find common ground. Any leader who wants to make changes is tempted to point out differences and try to convince others why change is needed. But that rarely works. Instead, focus on the similarities and build upon those. To get started, look for common ground in the following areas:

1. **Vision:** When the vision is similar, you can bet that the people are standing together and they have the same view. If their vision is similar to yours, you all see it clearly, and everyone has a strong desire to see it come to fruition.

2. **Values:** It's difficult to travel with others very long if your values don't align. Find out what others stand for and try to meet where you share the same standards.

3. **Relationships:** Great teams have people who are as committed to one another as they are to the vision.

4. **Attitude:** If you are going to get people to work together for positive change, their attitudes need to be positive and tenacious. If they're not, there will be trouble ahead.

5. **Communication:** For change to occur, communication must be open, honest, and ongoing. When people are in the dark, they start to speculate and make false assumptions about what's happening. Inform people so that everyone is on the same page.

After you establish common ground in these areas, you can start introducing actual changes. And it is usually up to leaders to initiate change. But here's the good news: If people need change, they tend to look to their leaders for inspiration and guidance. If you are ready to lead the charge for change, keep in mind the following guidelines:

Change What Needs to Be Changed, Not What Is Easy to Change

When organizations are having difficulties, leaders instinctively know that changes need to be made. One thing that isn't certain is whether they will introduce changes that make a difference, or merely cosmetic ones. Cosmetic changes are relatively easy to make. They give the semblance of change, but often don't actually produce positive results.

Changes that can make a difference are harder. Changing organizational culture when it's unhealthy, for example, is difficult. So is changing values, or leaders and the way they are developed. But these kinds of efforts are what really change an organization.

Let Go of Yesterday So You Can Move Toward Tomorrow

Because of the speed of change in technology today, people who work in that area accept that they must let go of yesterday and embrace change for the sake of tomorrow. Those of us who aren't technical or don't work in related industries seem to have a more difficult time with this concept. Bill Gates, cofounder and former CEO of Microsoft, once said, "In three years every product my company makes will be obsolete. The only question is whether we will make it obsolete or someone else will."

If you are going to lead change, you need to let go of outdated procedures and stale ideas, and you need to help the people you lead to do the same. That's often not just a practical or intellectual exercise; it's also an emotional one. Acknowledge the importance of the past. Honor the people who have made past contributions. But also show them why they can't stay where they are, and why the place you want to take them is so much better.

Communicate the Message with Simplicity and Power

There is great power in a simple and compelling message. As you communicate the vision for change, offer multiple reasons for it. The more reasons for change, the more likely people are to accept it. Certainly the main reason will probably be that it is better for the organization. But how is it also good for customers, clients, and the community? And how is it better for the people in the organization who must implement the change? Never underestimate the importance of answering the question "What's in it for me?"

Activate Belief in People

The first step to implementing any change is to believe in it yourself. Without your own conviction, you won't commit. People will sense that and will not follow you. But even more important than believing in the cause is belief in the people who will implement it. They will sense how much you believe in them, which will determine how willing they'll be to move forward. You energize an organization by energizing its people. Your belief activates their belief in themselves. Your confidence in them will give them confidence in themselves.

Remove Barriers for People

Once you communicate the need and vision for change and help people to believe they *can* change, your most important task as a leader is to start removing barriers that will keep people from executing the plan. Barriers are usually created by outdated systems, complicated procedures, difficult people, or strained resources. To find the barriers, get out among the people, watch what they're doing, and listen to their complaints. Ask yourself:

1. What internal barriers do I need to remove personally to help facilitate needed changes?
2. What policies are antithetical to the needed changes, and how can I remove them?
3. What unnecessary tasks can be eliminated to free people to implement the needed changes?
4. What resources can be freed up to help make the needed changes possible?
5. Who is trying to obstruct needed changes, and how can I get those people to change?

Lead with Speed

Never underestimate the significance of early victories for giving people confidence to keep moving forward. Success nourishes faith in the change effort. It gives an emotional lift to the people who are carrying and implementing the change. And it silences critics. Every success helps to build momentum, which is a leader's best friend.

Take Advantage of Momentum

Momentum helps a leader do anything and everything more easily. That's why I call it the great exaggerator. Without momentum, everything is harder to do than it should be. With it, everything is easier. Have it on your side, and your performance is actually better than your capability.

Momentum can make a significant difference in effecting change. When you and your people are powering through changes, momentum builds. Each change becomes easier because people are more comfortable with the process. And changes happen more quickly too.

You can jump-start momentum by offering small challenges to individual team members so that they experience individual wins. Then offer attainable challenges that people can win together as a team.

Push Past Obstacles

Everyone encounters obstacles in life. Teams face bigger ones as they move toward any goal. The obstacles faced by leaders are larger still. Especially in tough times, and while implementing change. They can take many forms, but here are some of the most common obstacles to change:

1. Failure

Perhaps the greatest challenge to change is failure. And failure is unavoidable. Olympic gold medalist Mary Lou Retton says, "Achieving that goal is a good feeling, but to get there you have to also get through the failures. You've got to be able to pick yourself up and continue."

2. Negativity Within the Ranks

Not everyone on your team will see change as a positive. Many will resist or try to avoid it. Others will challenge it more forcefully. Negativity can also appear when team members feel threatened by change. Seeing others change and grow may even demotivate some people. They see themselves being left behind, so they focus on the negative to slow down the process. And by the way, this isn't always intentional. Fear of change and risk can paralyze some people. But effective leaders attempt to reassure the fearful. If that doesn't work, they challenge the negativity and emphasize the benefits that will come with the change.

3. Deep Disappointment

Let's be honest, a lot of things can go wrong in implementing change. How will you react to those disappointments? How will your team? When failure happens, reframe it for yourself and your team. Search for something positive that you can obtain from the disappointment. At the very least, everyone can learn something from it.

Elevate Your Commitment

By now you know that the struggle is real. Leading your team over obstacles takes a great deal of determination. But that might not be enough on its own. It's not often an easy or speedy process. Force of will may not take you all the way through. You have to exercise commitment. Here are some tips for maximizing your ability to keep your commitment and clear a path forward:

Focus on Choices, Not Conditions

Some leaders look to conditions to determine whether they keep their commitments. But because conditions change, their commitment level changes like the wind. In contrast, those who base their actions on something internal usually focus on their choices. Each choice is a crossroads, one that will either confirm or compromise their commitments.

Crossroads have the following in common:

- A personal decision is required.
- The decision will cost you something.
- Others will likely be influenced by it.

Your choices are the only thing you truly control. You cannot control your circumstances, nor can you control other people. By focusing on your choices, and then making them with integrity, you confirm and strengthen your commitment. And that is what often separates success from failure.

Be Single-Minded

Nothing stokes commitment like single-minded effort that results in achievement. A great example of that truth can be found in the story of English minister William Carey. Although he had only an elementary education, he learned to read the Bible in six languages, became professor of Oriental languages at Fort William College in Calcutta, and became a publisher of Bibles in forty languages and dialects for more than three hundred million people. Carey attributed his success to being a "plodder." Describing himself, Carey said, "I can plod. That is my only genius. I can persevere in any definite pursuit. To this I owe everything."[3]

Do What's Right Even When You Don't Feel Like It

If you do what you should only when you feel like it, you won't keep your commitments. My friend Ken Blanchard says, "When you're interested in something, you do it only when it's convenient. When you're committed to something, you accept no excuses, only results." If you refuse to give in to excuses, no matter how good they may sound or how good they will make you feel in the moment, you will keep moving forward.

Always Strive for Excellence

Few things fire up a person's commitment like dedication to excellence. This is not the same as perfectionism, since that actually creates resistance to risk. Commitment to excellence motivates the team because the goal is clear. That doesn't mean you'll always reach it. But you will achieve much better results than the leader who aims for "good enough." Successful change is always more achievable when you need to set the bar high for yourself and your team. It's not enough to simply complete a task. Strive to perform it with excellence, without cutting any corners.

Grow Other Leaders

What is the best way to lead a large group of people through a tough change? Appoint other leaders to share the load. No leaders on your team? Then grow them. Investing in leaders offers a greater return than leading followers all by yourself. The more leaders you have, the stronger you are as a team. The better leaders an organization has, the greater its potential. Every time you increase the ability of a person in the group, you increase the team's ability to fulfill the vision. Everything gets better when good leaders are leading the organization.

How many times have you considered giving someone a task and instead thought, "It's easier to just do it myself"? Probably often. Why? Because it *is* easier. Doing the work yourself is always faster and easier than developing other people to do it. But to rely on your own ability and time to do everything is short-term thinking! Long-term thinking says it's better to take the time to equip people on the front end, because the return is great on the back end. Helping another person to become a competent leader almost always takes longer than you think and is more difficult than you expect. But when you do it, you expand the potential for yourself, your people, and your organization. When established leaders focus on people development and empower others to lead, everybody wins.

When new leaders are developed, they become better at what they do, and they help everyone who works with them to do the same. When these new leaders start building relationships with their people, they treat them better and the working environment improves, and with experience these new leaders also become more productive and help the team produce greater results. With the addition of more good leaders, the organization's current efforts improve. And expanding the leadership of the organization also gives it the ability to expand its territory, weather challenging times more effectively, and take on complicated changes.

✳   ✳   ✳

Regardless of the difficulties we may face, the principles of leadership remain steadfast. Helping others grow and develop brings joy, satisfaction, and energy to a leader, and it brings success to the team. Working together well toward a clear vision, each person utilizing personal strengths, lightens the burden for all. As you make changes, I challenge you to create a sense of community where victories are celebrated, gratitude is evident, and loyalty is shared. That is the sweetest result a leader can achieve.

3

The Teamwork Challenge

Building and Improving Your Team

Any organization that succeeds, in either easy or tough times, does so because of its people. It doesn't matter whether it's a small business, large corporation, sports team, nonprofit, or family. Organizationally, you live or die with your people.

Most of what an organization possesses goes down in value. Facilities deteriorate. Equipment becomes out of date. Supplies get used up. What asset has the greatest potential for actually going up in value? People! But only if they are valued, challenged, and developed by someone capable of investing in them and helping them grow. Otherwise, they are like money put on deposit without interest. Their potential is high, but they aren't actually growing. Appreciate your people as your greatest assets, and they will continually increase in value.

If you want to succeed in tough times, you need a better team. You need the right people in the right places doing the right things together. As the leader, you are responsible for facilitating these things.

Connect with Your Team

I think a lot of people don't take responsibility for the relationships in their lives. They simply let things happen to them rather than being intentional about it. But to have the kind of solid relationships that help you lead a strong team, you have to change your mind-set when it comes to dealing with others.

As a leader, you may be tempted to build relationships only with the people you like or with whom you are highly compatible, and to ignore the others. However, by doing that, you have the potential to lose a lot of people. It's important to remember that while the things we have in common may make relationships enjoyable, the differences are what really make them interesting. Good leaders deal successfully with these differences and leverage them for the benefit of the team and organization.

Here are some ways you can develop stronger relationships with each member of your team:

Place a High Value on Team Members

If you don't care about people, you are unlikely to make building good relationships a priority in your life. What onetime national salesman of the year Les Giblin said is true: "You can't make the other fellow feel important in your presence if you secretly feel that he is a nobody." The solution is to place a high value on people. Expect the best from everyone. Assume people's motives are good unless they prove them to be otherwise. Value them by their best moments. And give them your friendship rather than asking for theirs. That will ultimately be their decision.

Understand Each Person

Many people care about others, but they still remain out of touch. In those cases, I think the problem is that they don't understand people. If you desire to build positive relationships, then keep in mind the following truths about people—and actions you can take to bridge the gap often caused by them:

- People are insecure . . . give them confidence.
- People want to feel special . . . sincerely compliment them.

- People desire a better tomorrow...show them hope.
- People need to be understood...listen to them.
- People are selfish...speak to their needs first.
- People get emotionally low...encourage them.
- People want to be associated with success... help them win.

When you understand people, don't take their short-comings personally, and help them to succeed, you lay the groundwork for good relationships.

Give Respect Freely but Expect to Earn It from Others

I believe every human being deserves to be treated with respect because everyone has value. People who disrespect others always hurt themselves relationally—and they often reap other negative consequences. Giving people respect first is one of the most effective ways of interacting with others. However, that doesn't mean you can demand respect in return. You must earn it. If you respect yourself, respect others, and exhibit competence, others will almost always give you respect.

Make Other People's Agendas Your Priority

Too many leaders think that leadership is only about their own agenda. Good leaders focus on the needs and wants of their people, and as far as it is within their power, they make their people's hopes and dreams a priority. Just by virtue of listening and remembering what's important to them, you communicate that you care and desire to add value. There is great power when the vision of the organization and the dreams of its people come into alignment, and everybody wins.

Commit Yourself to Their Growth

Some people approach every interaction with others as a transaction. They're willing to add value, but only if they expect to receive value in return. If you want to make relationships a priority, you must check your motives to be sure you are not trying to manipulate others for your own gain. The best way to add value to others is to ...

- Look for ability in others.
- Help others discover their ability.
- Help others develop their ability.

Nothing lifts a person like being respected and valued by others. As a leader, you should make sure your goals include becoming aware of the uniqueness of people and learning to appreciate their differences. You need to let them know that they matter, that you see them as individual human beings, not just workers. This attitude makes a positive impact on people, and it strengthens your leadership.

There is no downside to adding value to people. Yes, it will cost you time and effort. But when you add value to people, you help them and make them more valuable. If you're a leader, when your people are on purpose and content, you help your team. When your team is more effective, you help your organization because it becomes better. And the whole process will bring you a deep sense of satisfaction.

Good relationships create energy, and they give people's interaction a positive tone. When you invest time and effort to get to know people and build good relationships, it actually pays off with greater energy once the relationships are built. And in that kind of positive, energetic environment, people are willing to give their best because they know the leader wants the best for them.

Build a Stronger Team

Author Stephen R. Covey asserted, "The basic role of the leader is to foster mutual respect and build a complementary team where each strength is made productive and each weakness made irrelevant."[4] That is the ideal that every leader should shoot for—people working together, each bringing their strengths to make the team better and compensating for each other's weaknesses. When you really get to know your people, you will be able to identify where they add the greatest value to the team. Take some time to define each team member's area of contribution (including your own), and figure out how you all work together to make the team most effective.

Developing a group of people into a productive team is no easy task. It's a challenge to get everybody working together to achieve a common vision. Sometimes that requires moving people around to find where they make the greatest contribution. Sometimes it means trying and failing. As a leader, you have to take it all in stride. Positioning people correctly is a process, and you have to treat it that way. But if you don't do it, you will never help your people reach their potential. It is definitely worth the effort. Being part of a team of people doing something of high value is one of the most rewarding experiences in life. As a leader, you have a chance to help people experience it. Don't shrink from that great opportunity.

Spend time getting to know what each person can

do. Evaluate their present skills, potential capacities, level of commitment, ability to be motivated, discipline, and intensity. Only then can you discover the best way to motivate, develop, position, and equip your team. During this process, you'll likely discover people who do not push themselves to their full capacity. If you lead people who are falling short of their potential, you need to start asking why. Have you put them in their strength zones? Are you providing the training and resources they need to be successful? Is there something they need that you're not giving? You always need to make sure you are not the problem before you look to see where the problem is.

Many people don't have a greater vision for their lives. And it's easy for people, even those who want to grow, to get into a rut and stay in their comfort zone. As a leader you should try to encourage them to move forward and reach for their potential. You're not responsible for their response. Every individual has to take responsibility for that. But you can model growth, encourage them, and try to be a catalyst for positive change. Here's how:

1. Show Them a Vision for Their Better Future

If people cannot see a better future for themselves, you need to show it to them. Start by asking them questions: If you could be anything you wanted, what would you be? If you could do anything you wanted, what would you do? If you knew you could not fail, what would you try? See what stirs inside them. Many people have dreams deep inside that need only a bit of encouragement to coax out.

2. Treat Them Not as They Are, but as They Could Be

If you were to treat the people around you as they could be instead of as they are, how do you think they would respond? If they've been in a rut a long time, they might not rise up right away. You might have to keep speaking positively about them and treating them as people who desire to reach their potential, but I believe that in time most would rise up. Give it a try. Speak positively about a better future for them, and they just might try to live up to it.

3. Set Them Up for a Win

Many times people aren't willing to leave their comfort zone because they are convinced that they cannot win. But as a leader, you proactively set people up for success and help them achieve a win so that they gain confidence and experience. If you put them in a position where a win is almost guaranteed, they can have that winning experience inspire them to move forward.

Remember it is their choice, not yours. You can't push people to reach their potential. You can choose to leave the door open for them, but they must walk through. If they choose not to, you're better off spending your time on the team members who actively want to grow. But sometimes all people need is some encouragement. We are all capable of doing more and going higher than we believe we can.

Create a Culture of Unity

If you have waited for people on your team to come to you for leadership, you need to change your approach to connecting with them. Get out of your office or cubicle and initiate contact with them. Make a sincere effort to get to know them, express your appreciation to them, encourage them, and offer your support to them. Make it your goal to add value to each person and promote teamwork. Here are my suggestions for adding value:

Promote Full Commitment

A team whose members aren't committed is doomed to perform unevenly when the heat is on. That commitment must start with the leader and extend to the entire team. If you are a leader, the true measure of your success is not getting people to work. It's not getting people to work hard. It is getting people to work hard together. That takes commitment.

Create an Environment of Encouragement and Support

One of the nicest things about teamwork is that you always have others on your side. It's pulling together, not pulling apart. It's many voices, one heart. But that often doesn't occur unless there is an environment of encouragement and support. Leaders need to take responsibility for working to create that. People look for and thrive on acknowledgment and appreciation. Encourage each person to take some time and come up with positive things that they can honestly say about everyone else. Then challenge them to share those comments with each other. When people believe in themselves, they perform better. In general, people rise to the level of expectations. If you see the value in everyone and let them know that you value them, it helps them, it helps the organization, and it helps you as a leader.

Reframe Adversity and Failure as Opportunities to Develop Character

Teamwork is never tested during good times. You know how good your team is when adversity hits. It introduces you to yourself, and it reveals where you're strong and where you're weak. We often don't like that, but the reality is that losses can be learning experiences if your attitude is right. Author and apologist C. S. Lewis took that thought one step further. He wrote, "God allows us to experience the low points of life in order to teach us lessons we could not learn in any other way." We would be wise to look for the opportunity in adversity and learn from it.

Remind Them to Stay Focused on the Team

Many people naturally focus on themselves. Who is the first person you look for when you see a group picture? Yourself. How do you determine if it's a good picture? It usually depends on how good you look in it. Only after you've checked your own image do you begin looking at everyone else's. Teamwork demands that we focus a little less on ourselves and a little more on how the team looks. You can do that by asking, "What's best for the rest?"

Help Each Other Until the Vision Is Accomplished

It's one thing to say you want to help people on your team. It's another to actually follow through and assist them all along the way. Talk to them about ways to help them accomplish their vision while they do their work and help the organization. Then, together, formulate a plan to help them do it. When you follow through, you not only help them, you also build your leadership credibility and your influence, with them and with everyone else on the team.

Hold Team Members Accountable

Anytime you have difficulty with a person you lead, whether it's because of a negative attitude, poor performance, lack of cooperation, or some other issue, you need to start a process right away, and that process is the same for nearly every situation. Before I lay it out for you, I want to point out two questions you need to ask before you get started:

Can this person change? This deals with ability.
Will this person change? This deals with attitude.

Often the problem does not relate to ability but to attitude. But for this process to be successful, when you ask a person to change, the answer to both questions has to be yes. It can't be either/or. I've known people with great ability but a bad attitude, and I've known people with a great attitude and poor ability. If the person is able and willing to change, there's a chance you can be successful.

1. Meet Privately ASAP to Discuss Their Behavior

If you have a problem with someone, do something about it as quickly as you can. Meet with the person privately and level with them with integrity and honesty. Never go into one of these meetings angry. If you do, you greatly reduce your chances of success.

Sit down and very clearly lay out what the issue is, giving specific, tangible examples of the undesirable actions or behaviors. Don't be vague. Don't use secondhand reports. Don't attribute bad motives to them, because they will only get defensive. In fact, go into the conversation assuming their motives are good. This is more likely to make them open to change and willing to make corrections. And be sure to explain how their actions are negatively affecting the organization, the team, or you.

2. Ask for Their Side of the Story

I'm a pretty good judge of people, but I still sometimes read situations wrong. I misunderstand something that happened, make wrong assumptions, or don't realize I'm missing an important piece of information. Sometimes circumstances, such as a personal tragedy, are temporarily prompting unwanted behavior, and the person simply needs help or understanding. That's why you don't want to go in with guns blazing. You might be wrong.

3. Try to Come to a Place of Agreement

At this point it's time to find out if they agree with you. If they do agree, it can be very humbling for them, but it opens them up to change, and that's ideal. Often you can help someone with that attitude.

If they disagree, perhaps say it's someone else's problem, I tell them, "I believe I'm right and this is your problem. I'm going to give you a week to think about it. We'll meet again and discuss it." My hope is that they'll give it some honest thought and maybe ask people who know them well and will be honest with them.

If they have a change of heart after a week, we can move forward to the next step because they've taken responsibility. If they still don't agree, I say, "You may not agree with what I've just said. But you will have to agree to change and follow my guidelines if you want to remain on the team. And I'm going to hold you accountable."

4. Set Out a Future Course of Action with a Deadline

No matter whether the person agrees with you or not, you must lay out a specific course of action for them to take. Indicate any actions they must not take or behaviors they must not exhibit, starting immediately. If there are action steps they will need to follow through on, lay those out and put deadlines on them. And make sure they understand. Put your requirements into writing if needed. If you don't both agree on what needs to happen in the future, you will both be frustrated.

5. Validate the Value of the Person and Express Your Commitment to Help

Before you finish your meeting, let them know that you care about them and genuinely desire a positive resolution to the situation. Tell them how you will help them. Goethe recommended, "Treat people as if they were what they ought to be, and you help them become what they are capable of becoming."

Sometimes the greatest value a leader can add to other people comes through telling them the truth, showing them where they can grow, and then helping them change. Some people spend years on a job being resented by their boss and fellow employees, but are never told about their problem or given a chance to change and grow. As a leader, you have the chance to help them.

Sitting down with people and telling them where they fall short isn't easy. And there's no guarantee that they will acknowledge their problem or change. There's a chance that you will have to let them go. If you are having a hard time making that decision, ask yourself this question: "If I needed to hire new people, knowing what I know now, would I hire these individuals?"

If the answer is yes—keep them.

If the answer is no—let them go.

If the answer is maybe—reevaluate in three months.

If after three months you still don't know if it's yes or no, the answer is really no. Your emotions are making it difficult for you to accept a hard decision. Ultimately, as a leader, you owe it to the rest of the team to make these tough choices. That's what you get paid for.

✳   ✳   ✳

Leaders who think they must work alone, standing atop the hill of leadership while their subordinates work together at the bottom, have teams that work far under their capabilities. Stand-alone leadership doesn't lead to teamwork, creativity, collaboration, or high achievement. Good leadership is about leading *with* others, not just leading others. It requires collaboration. It requires inclusion. It requires sacrifice of selfish personal ambition for the sake of the team and the vision of the organization. Put others ahead of yourself and you will be part of something greater than yourself.

4

The Motivation Challenge

Inspiring Your Team to Excellence

Let's face it. Tough times can be discouraging. People can lose confidence and start believing the worst about themselves, their team, and their circumstances. Leaders can help their teams through these difficulties. They can create energy and inspire others to achieve. During tough times, your job is to motivate your team to keep moving forward despite the obstacles in their path. As a leader, not only do you have the responsibility for the success of your team, you are in the position to inspire people to excel in spite of what you are all facing.

Check Your Motives

Someone once said, "People have two reasons for doing anything—a good reason and the real reason." For you to be a good leader, the good reason must be the same as the real reason. Your motives matter. It's easy for a leader to lose focus. That's why you need to check your motives daily.

Naturally gifted leaders have capabilities that they can easily use for personal advantage. They see things before others do, and they often see more than others see. As a result, they enjoy the advantage of having good timing and seeing the big picture. That puts them in a position to make the most of opportunities.

If I can see something before you do, I can get started before you, and that often guarantees a win. If I see more than you see, my decisions will likely be better than yours. I win again! So the question is not "Does the leader have an advantage over others?" The answer to that question is yes. The question is "Will the leader use that advantage for personal gain or for the benefit of everyone on the team?" That is why you need to ask yourself whether you are genuinely interested in others. It will keep any natural selfishness in check and purify your motives.

Questioning your motives is not the same as questioning your character. If you have poor character, your motives will probably be bad. But if you have solid character, you can still fall prey to bad motives. Motives are usually attached to specific situations or actions. Character is based on values. If you have wrong motives in a particular situation, but your values are good and your character is strong, you will probably detect where you're going wrong and have a chance to correct it.

Model Your Own Motivation

Leadership isn't easy. Every day, leaders must wake up and lead themselves before they lead anyone else. Because other people are depending on them, they must keep the fire burning within themselves. They must know where they're going, know why they're going, and help others get there. Some leaders make the same mistake as some parents. They expect people to do as they say, not as they do. But here's the problem: People do what people see. If you want dedicated, motivated, productive people on your team, you must model those characteristics.

Take time to list all the qualities you desire in your

team members. Then compare your own personal qualities to those on the list. Wherever you don't measure up, next to the characteristic write an action statement describing what you must do to possess the trait you'd like to see. For example, if you want people to be dedicated, then write, "I will not give up solving a problem or doing a task until it is completed," or, "I will arrive early and stay late to set an example for the team."

Too many leaders disconnect. They have a been-there-done-that mentality that is alienating, not alluring. In contrast, if you have a been-there-love-that way of thinking, people will be attracted to you and want to do their best when they engage with you.

Check Your Own Passion for the Work

You can stay energized and on course by tapping into three areas:

1. **Passion:** Passion gives you two vital leadership characteristics: energy and credibility. When you love what you do and do what you love, others find it inspiring.

2. **Principles:** Successful leaders stay true to their principles—to their beliefs, gifts, and personality. They don't try to lead in a style that does not suit who they are. Their leadership style is

comfortable and reflects who they truly are. The better you know yourself and the more true you are to yourself, the greater your potential for sustainable success.

3. **Practices:** Successful leaders do daily what unsuccessful people do occasionally. They practice daily disciplines. They implement systems for their personal growth. They make it a habit to maintain a positive attitude. At the very least, these things keep their personal momentum going. At their very best, they make every day a masterpiece.

To identify and implement your own daily practices, try starting with what I call my daily dozen:

Just for today . . .
I will choose and display the right attitudes.
I will determine and act upon important priorities.
I will know and follow healthy guidelines.
I will communicate with and care for my family.
I will practice and develop good thinking.
I will make and keep proper commitments.
I will earn and properly manage finances.
I will deepen and live out my faith.
I will initiate and invest in solid relationships.
I will plan for and model generosity.

I will embrace and practice good values.
I will seek and experience improvements.

By working toward these goals, not only will you ground yourself to weather difficult times, you will inspire your team to move forward and improve through your example.

Build and Maintain Trust

Author and pastor Rick Warren observed, "You can impress people from a distance, but you must get close to influence them." When you do that, they can see your flaws. However, Warren notes, "The most essential quality for leadership is not perfection but credibility. People must be able to trust you."

Most people don't want to admit their mistakes, expose their faults, and face up to their shortcomings. They don't want to be discovered. They don't get too close to people because of the negatives in their lives. They believe they must show greater strength as leaders and hide their weaknesses. However, if leaders try to maintain a facade with the people they lead, they cannot build authentic relationships.

To gain the trust of their people, leaders need to be authentic. They must admit their mistakes. They must own up to their faults. They must recognize their short-comings. In other words, they must be the real deal. That is a vulnerable place to be for a leader.

Trust is one of the foundations of effective leadership. If you have integrity with people, you develop trust. The more trust you develop, the stronger the relationship becomes. The better the relationship, the greater the potential that the person will be motivated to follow you. It's a building process that takes time, energy, and intentionality.

Retired admiral James Stockdale said, "When the crunch comes, people cling to those they know they can trust—those who are not detached, but involved." In times of difficulty, relationships are a shelter. In times of opportunity, they are a launching pad. Trust is required for people to feel safe enough to create, share, question, attempt, and risk. Without it, leadership is weak and teamwork is impossible.

Here are three ways you can develop trust between you and your team:

1. Practice the Golden Rule

It takes a leap of faith to put your trust in another person, especially someone you don't know well. But practicing the Golden Rule is a good way to start. Strive to invest confidence in others in the same way you would like it invested in you. Camillo Benso di Cavour said, "The man who trusts men will make fewer mistakes than he who distrusts them."

2. Place High Value on People

Trust is a two-way street. If you want your team to trust you, you need to trust them. That means you must value others enough to give them your trust. In *Winning Management: 6 Fail-Safe Strategies for Building High-Performance Organizations*, Wolf J. Rinke writes, "If you mistrust your employees, you'll be right 3 percent of the time. If you trust people until they give you a reason not to, you'll be right 97 percent of the time."[5] Those are pretty good odds.

3. Take Responsibility for Your Actions

If you desire to be trusted by others and you want to achieve much, you must take responsibility for your actions. A person of responsibility can trust himself to choose the right thing over the easy thing. Winston Churchill was right when he called responsibility "the price of greatness." It's also the groundwork for opportunity.

While you cannot control whether people give you their trust, you can control your actions toward them. And you can determine to give them *your* trust.

Create a Culture of Motivation

When I started out in leadership, I thought I could change people. Now I realize I can't. People must change themselves. That doesn't mean that I have no responsibility to people in my organization in the area of motivation. There are still things I can do. I can work to create an environment and culture where motivation is valued and rewarded. Here are the ways I do that:

Start with Motivated People

The best way to create a culture of motivation is to start with as many motivated people as you can. The Law of Magnetism in *The 21 Irrefutable Laws of Leadership* states, "Who you are is who you attract." As discussed, if you want people on your team to be motivated, you must be motivated yourself. People do what people see. I have to live it before I expect it from anyone else.

You should also hire motivated people. That sounds obvious, but you might be surprised how many leaders leave this trait out of the equation when looking for team members. Many focus too much on just talent or skill. Even the leaders who recognize the importance of attitude sometimes miss motivation. And then they wonder why their people aren't performing at a higher level.

How can you identify motivated people? They usually have several of the following traits:

1. They exhibit a positive attitude.
2. They can articulate specific goals for their life.
3. They are initiators.
4. They have a proven track record of success.

Look for these traits when looking for new team members.

People are motivated by leaders who connect with them and treat them like human beings. If you are a people person, this may sound painfully obvious to you, yet some leaders still miss it. I once knew a leader who referred to all the people on his team as "ding-a-lings." He was constantly saying things like "I told the ding-a-lings what to do, but of course they didn't do it" and "I've got to go meet with the ding-a-lings." It was clear that he believed everyone was below him. His contempt for people was apparent to everyone who worked for him. Few things are more demotivating than working for someone who disrespects you.

Share Your Passion

If you have passion for what you do, you need to share it with your people. A leader's passion is contagious. It can attract other passionate people, and it can spark a flame in people who might not otherwise be passionate. If they can understand and connect with the vision you have and the passion you feel, there's a good chance that they will catch it and become passionate too.

Paint a Picture of a Better Future

As I already mentioned, a job is never big enough for people. They want to do something bigger, something that is worth working for. People want to make a difference. One of your jobs as a leader is to paint a picture of their future that inspires them to work harder today. Tell them who they can become. Show them what they could someday be doing. This must be done with integrity, because as leaders, we never want to manipulate people. We just want to help them envision the future.

Show How Their Role Makes a Difference

Too often people don't understand how the tasks they do contribute to the bigger picture. Good leaders help team members understand their role. They help them see how their contribution is making a difference. This gives team members a sense of ownership over the mission and inspires them to do better work.

Give Each Person a Reputation to Uphold

People often go farther than they think they can go when someone else thinks they can. One way to show people that you believe in them and in the possibility of success for their future is to give them a reputation to uphold.

Ask yourself what's special, unique, and wonderful about each person on your team. All people have talents, skills, and positive traits that make them valuable to the team. Figure out what they are and then share them with others. The more you validate people for the good things they do—or could do—the more they want to do them. Not only does this motivate them to perform in their strength, it also encourages an environment where people say positive things about one another.

Reward What You Want Done

If you want to create an environment where people are motivated, give them reasons to get things done. I love the story of the salesman who sat looking through the window of a hotel restaurant. Outside raged a blinding snowstorm.

"Do you think the roads will be clear enough in the morning to travel?" he asked his waiter.

"That depends," the waiter replied. "Are you on salary or commission?"

Rewards are motivating. Rules, consequences, and punishment don't do anything to get people going. They merely keep people from doing their worst. If you want people's best, give them incentives for performance.

Challenge Them to Keep Growing

H. Nelson Jackson said, "I do not believe you can do today's job with yesterday's methods and be in business tomorrow." That's why we need to help people see the value of growing. It is essential not only for the organization's viability, but also for the individual's future. People who make growth their goal—instead of a title, position, salary, or other external target—always have a future.

Maintain Motivation

Some people may start out strong, ambitious, innovative, and motivated, but they don't always stay that way. This is particularly true if you don't build and maintain a good relationship with them. If you are not effective at motivating your team, they often become one of three types of people:

Clock Watchers

Unmotivated workers love clocks and they want them visible at all times. Why? Because every moment at work is evaluated according to the clock. Clock watchers always know how much time is left before they get to go home, and they never want to work a moment beyond quitting time. But think about it: When the people who work with you can hardly wait to quit working with you, something is not working!

Just-Enough Employees

Some people do just enough—to get by, to get paid, and to keep their job. For them, the big question is not "What can I do to be a valuable employee?" but "How much must I do to be an employee?" They don't ask, "How can I advance and get promoted?" They only ask, "How can I keep from getting fired?" They give reluctant compliance, not commitment. Some spend a lot of mental energy finding creative ways of eliminating work. If only they used that commitment in positive ways!

The Mentally Absent

In an environment that lacks effective leadership, there are always individuals who may be physically present but mentally absent. They show up merely to collect a paycheck. This attitude is highly damaging to an organization because it seems to spread. When one person checks out mentally and doesn't receive any consequences for it, others often follow them. When the people who work for a team, a department, or an organization give little of themselves, the results are mediocre at best. And morale is abysmal.

If people see the work they're currently doing as nothing more than a job for a paycheck, they will become frustrated over time. Almost equally frustrating is targeting a particular position or title and then thinking you've arrived once you receive it. No *job* has a future. Only *people* have a future. If people keep growing, learning, and expanding their potential, their future is bright. If not, it's uncertain at best. That's why I often remind people that the greatest threat to tomorrow's success is today's success.

If you're leading people who have settled into a role or position, whether it's because they are in a comfort zone or because they see their work as just a job, try to help them open their eyes and think beyond today. Remind them that a job is never big enough for a human being. We have too much inside us for that.

Keep Increasing Motivation Through Encouragement

I have yet to meet a person who doesn't enjoy and benefit from encouragement. No one is too successful, old, experienced, or educated to appreciate positive praise and encouragement from another person. As a leader, you have great power to lift people up. Mother Teresa said, "Kind words can be short and easy to speak, but their echoes are endless." As a leader, you can have a positive impact on others. People enjoy affirmation from a peer. But they really value it from their leader. The words *I'm glad you work with me; you add incredible value to the team* mean a lot coming from someone who has the best interest of the team, department, or organization at heart.

If you want people to be positive and to always be glad when they see you coming, encourage them. If you become the chief encourager of the people on your team, they will work hard and strive to meet your positive expectations. Try it out. For the next two weeks, say something encouraging to someone on your team every day. Then watch to see how the person responds. Do that with everyone on your team, and not only will they want to work with you, but they will also get more done.

All of these things have the potential to help a leader

inspire someone to invest himself more fully in his work and stop coasting. But remember everything I've just discussed rests on one assumption: that you are passionate about your own work. That is essential. People do not follow an uncertain trumpet. They can't catch fire from a leader who has grown cold himself. If you aren't fired up, you are a big part of the problem, and the first person you must motivate is yourself.

✽ ✽ ✽

President Theodore Roosevelt is often quoted as saying, "The best executive is the one who has sense enough to pick good men to do what he wants done, and self-restraint enough to keep from meddling with them while they do it." What he's describing is empowerment. That's helping people to see what they can do without your help, and releasing them to do it.

When you believe in people, you motivate them. Draw upon the experiences you have with your team and the growth that they have already exhibited. Highlight their wins. Celebrate victories with them. And show them you care. Few things put wind in another person's sails like your faith in them.

5

The Strategy Challenge

Discovering New Ways to Win

Psychiatrist M. Scott Peck said, "Life is a series of problems. Do we want to moan about them or solve them?" During tough times, the strategy challenge for leaders is finding new ways to win because, to paraphrase Albert Einstein, we cannot solve our problems with the same thinking that created them.

Facing Tough Challenges

The key to overcoming challenges is to approach them the right way. Over the years, I've learned that difficulties get better or worse based on what you do or don't do when you face them. First, let me give you the don'ts:

1. Don't Underestimate the Challenge

Many difficulties go unresolved or are managed ineffectively because we do not take them seriously enough. Years ago I read a wonderful book by Robert H. Schuller entitled *Tough Times Never Last, but Tough People Do!* The following paragraphs helped me as a young leader to find a more realistic view of my problems and myself:

> Never underestimate a problem or your power to cope with it. Realize that the problem you are facing has been faced by millions of human beings. You have untapped potential for dealing with a problem if you will take the problem and your own undeveloped, unchanneled powers seriously. Your reaction to the problem, as much as the problem itself, will determine the outcome.
>
> I have seen people face the most catastrophic problems with a positive mental attitude, turning their problems into creative experiences. They turned their scars into stars.[6]

When I first read those paragraphs, I became inspired. It made me believe that the size of the person is more important than the size of the problem.

2. Don't Overestimate the Challenge

Cy Young was one of the greatest pitchers in Major League Baseball. After his career was over, he commented on the tendencies of managers to take their starters out of the game at the slightest hint of trouble. He observed, "In our day, when a pitcher got into trouble in a game, instead of taking him out, our manager would leave him in and tell him to pitch his way out of trouble." Sometimes the problem is not as big a problem as we anticipate, and by tackling it, we shrink it down in size.

3. Don't Wait for the Challenge to Solve Itself

That brings us to the next lesson I've learned about challenges. You can't wait for them to solve themselves. Patience is a virtue in problem solving if you are at the same time doing all that you can to fix the situation. It is not a virtue if you are simply waiting, hoping that the problem will solve itself or just go away.

Problems demand that we pay them attention. Why? Because left alone they almost always get worse. Nina DiSesa, who led the ad agency McCann Erickson in the late 1990s, observed, "When you step into a turnaround situation, you can safely assume four things: Morale is low, fear is high, the good people are halfway out the door, and the slackers are hiding." Those things won't improve on their own. They require intentional problem solving and active leadership.

Do These Things

Instead, face your challenges and do these things as you prepare to develop your strategy.

1. Face the Challenge

They say the punch that knocks you out is not necessarily the hardest one, but the one you didn't see coming. As a leader, you have to face up to the challenge, really look it in the eye—no matter how ugly it might be.

2. Understand the Challenge

Whenever I'm preparing to develop a strategy, I first try to gather information and find out people's experiences and perspectives. That process helps me to better understand what's going on and where everyone is coming from. Sometimes I find out that the challenge we have isn't the challenge I thought it was. Occasionally, I discover that the problem I was concerned about wasn't actually a problem at all. When you are facing challenges, it's crucial that you get the entire team on the same page and work on it together.

3. Evaluate the Challenge

Once you have done your due diligence in gathering information, you need to ask yourself, "What is the issue?" Can you discern the heart of the challenge?

The second question you need to ask is "Who is involved?" Are the people connected to this challenge making it more or less difficult to deal with?

As you evaluate challenges, try to maintain perspective, and always keep the end in mind. I saw something when I lived in southern Indiana that captures this idea concisely. It was a sign on a farm fence that read IF YOU CROSS THIS FIELD YOU HAD BETTER DO IT IN 9.8 SECONDS. THE BULL CAN DO IT IN 10 SECONDS.

4. Appreciate the Challenge

Appreciating a challenge is counterintuitive for many people. Most people see every problem as a nuisance and try to avoid it. However, if we have the right attitude and appreciate a problem, not only will we work harder to solve it, but we will also learn and grow from it. Remember, challenges always bring opportunities, and opportunities always bring challenges. The two go hand in hand. If we can learn to appreciate that truth, we have a real advantage in life.

Be Willing to Take Risks

As you begin to develop new strategies in tough times, face individual challenges, and work as an agent of change, you will have to take risks. So will your team. As Nobel Prize–winning writer William Faulkner said, "You cannot swim for new horizons until you have courage to lose sight of the shore."

While you prepare to manage the risks of developing winning strategies and pursuing them, keep these thoughts in mind:

1. Reality Is Your Friend During High-Risk Times

Businessman and author Max De Pree said that the first responsibility of a leader is to define reality. That's true for anyone striking out to win during tough times. Since it involves taking big risks, you can't depend on hype or wishful thinking, because those things cannot withstand the heat of risk. You need to understand what you're dealing with, look at the worst-case scenarios, and look reality dead in the eye.

How do you look reality in the face when evaluating a risk? Ask yourself some questions:

Who else has done it?

How bad can it get?

How good can it get?

Can I try it on for size?

How much room for error is there?

Does the past say yes?

Is there enough momentum to make it?

Do I believe in myself?

Do I believe in my team?

The more questions you ask and answer, the better prepared you are to weigh the risk and gauge whether the risk is smart or foolish.

2. *Good Leaders Learn to Be Comfortable Outside of Their Comfort Zone*

Risk is rarely comfortable. It requires us to get out of our comfort zone. Yet that's where we need to live in order to make changes and develop winning strategies. How do you deal with that? For me, anything worthwhile that I've ever done initially scared me to death. First speech? Frightened beyond belief. First board meeting? Scared stiff. Officiating my first wedding? I almost fainted! I was never good the first time, and I was always scared on top of that.

I love the way author and writing guru Steven

Pressfield says this: "The amateur believes he must first overcome his fear; then he can do his work. The professional knows that fear can never be overcome." Since you can't defeat fear or feel comfortable with it, you have to learn to deal with it. I call this becoming comfortable outside of your comfort zone.

3. Good Leadership Gives You a Greater Chance for Success

The statement I'm probably known for more than any other is this: Everything rises and falls on leadership. That is never truer than during times of risk. The size of the leadership must be equal to the size of the risk. If you're going to attempt something difficult, you need good leadership. You need to either provide it yourself or find a partner who can help you lead. And if you're going to try something huge, you'll need lots of leaders. Any great attempt without great leadership is destined to fizzle out.

4. The Bigger the Risk, the More Help You'll Need from Others

While it's fun to dream about the potential of winning during a time of challenge, the reality of it can make us want to yell, "Help!" at the top of our lungs. The greater and riskier the venture, the more our need for help. And to be successful, you don't just need help; you need the right kind of help. What are the characteristics of the right people?

They Like a Challenge

For years I've maintained that winners stretch to a challenge and whiners shrink from a challenge. When you cast vision for something big, it is both a uniter and divider. People of high capacity who like a challenge rally to you. Small people leave. The size of the vision determines the size of the person who signs up. Do you want to attract bigger people? Challenge them.

They Play Big

Nelson Mandela said, "There is no passion to be found playing small—in settling for a life that's less than the one you are capable of living." I know there are people who believe that playing big is dangerous, but do you want to know what's more dangerous? Never taking a risk. When you're doing nothing, nothing good happens.

They Are Honest with Themselves

When you're taking big risks and tackling challenges during tough times, you want people on your team who know themselves and are honest with themselves. They have to know what they're capable of and understand the stakes. And as a leader, you need to help make sure they know those things.

No matter how great or small your leadership responsibilities, you will need help when you take a risk. Look for like-minded people who are willing to face challenges to assist you. It will greatly increase your chances of success.

5. *Taking Risks Always Requires Personal Courage*

Writer Anaïs Nin said, "Life shrinks or expands in proportion to one's courage." If you want to succeed in tough times, you need to be willing to take greater risks. You need to be willing to stand alone. You need to gather the courage to do what others might not do— not just for the sake of doing something bold and risky, but because you can see the potential reward for your organization or team.

What's great about taking smart risks is that it not only expands your possibilities, but it also inspires other people to join you in your efforts. People follow courage. When someone is willing to stand up and face a challenge in the beginning, they earn respect and credibility. Eventually, others appreciate their courage and rally around them.

It's been said that if you're not living on the edge, you are taking up too much room. Risk is an important part of the strategy challenge for a leader.

Pursue a Winning Strategy

My friend and associate Paul Martinelli is a fantastic strategic thinker. He loves a challenge, and over the course of his life he's developed a fantastic process that has made him highly successful. I want to share Paul's principles with you. They can be applied to any kind of challenge whether you are leading a business, a non-profit organization, a home remodel, a sports team— you name it. If you want to increase your chances for winning, take these ideas to heart:

1. Visualize the Perfect Outcome

Stephen R. Covey advised in *The 7 Habits of Highly Effective People* that we should always begin with the end in mind. Paul takes this idea one step further. He calls this "creating a mental model of perfection." He doesn't just want to know where he's going. He wants to visualize the *perfect* outcome with as much detail as he possibly can.

Do you have a vision for what you want to accomplish? Have you created a mental model of perfection for what you desire to achieve? If not, you need to work on that. It's your starting point. Put as much detail to it as you can. Will the results actually *be* perfect? No. But that process is where you need to start.

2. Start Working Before You Know How to Achieve the Vision

When you want to accomplish something, you have to have a vision for what you're trying to do, but you also have to be willing to take action in the face of uncertainty. You need to tap into your thinking capacity to know what you're shooting for, but you also need to have a bias for action to be productive. You have to be willing to take a step, probably a small step.

Most people want to start with one bold, certain leap. They want a big head start, a quantum leap. But quantum leaps are rare. If we're willing to take one small step, ten small steps, one hundred small steps, then we may have a chance to make a leap later. It may look like an overnight success to others, but we'll know it's the result of many small successes. And you don't achieve those unless you're willing to take that *first* uncertain step.

3. Fail Fast, Fail First, and Fail Often

This next step also seems to fly in the face of the idea of aiming for a perfect outcome. To make progress, you have to be willing to fail. That's the best way to keep things moving, which is important in the face of a challenge.

Are you willing to fail? Are you willing to fail repeatedly? Are you willing to learn from what didn't work? That's what will be required for you to win.

4. Stop Doing What You're Not Great at Doing

You will drastically increase your results if you stop doing what you're not great at and instead focus on what you do best. Find ways to focus your team on the things that have a high return and eliminate anything that doesn't.

5. Tune In to Your Team Every Day

The people on your team determine whether or not you will be successful. They are the closest to the action, know best what's happening, and are most likely able to identify what's working and what isn't. For those reasons, become highly intentional in staying connected to your people.

You can do this by visiting their workspaces, walking through the halls, having dinner with them, or taking them with you to events. Those closest to you determine your level of success, so maintain and develop those relationships. Add value to your team members whenever you can.

6. Make Decisions Every Day to Move Yourself and the Team Forward

We'll discuss decision making in greater depth in the last chapter, so I'll be brief here. When you're willing to start small and without a surefire plan, you have to be willing to make adjustments continually. In these early stages, make your decisions based on whether or not they move the team forward or backward in the journey toward the vision, not on whether they are right or wrong. When it comes to character and ethical decisions, yes, there is a right and wrong. But when it comes to productivity and achievement, there isn't. Either something works or it doesn't. Either it takes you forward, or it doesn't. If you develop the habit of making quick decisions and trying new things, then evaluating whether or not they took you forward and adjusting as needed, you will make progress during tough times.

7. Continually Reevaluate What Could Work Better

Successful leaders are always working to become better and to find better ways of doing things. They are motivated by continual improvement. Paul Martinelli says, "We have three options in life. We can be historians, reporters, or futurists. The historian wants to remind us of everything in the past and wants to filter everything in the future through that. The reporter is really attached to conditions and circumstances today, and that's just the way it is. The futurist focuses on what hasn't yet been done. He says, 'There is more for us to do. We can do more. We can broaden our capacity. There is more of our potential we can take advantage of.'"

The only time you really control is now. You can't change yesterday. You can't control tomorrow. But you can choose today's actions with the intention of making things better tomorrow. Professor Edward Banfield of Harvard University confirmed the importance of a future focus in his book *The Unheavenly City*. He called it a "long-term perspective," and said that according to studies, it is the most accurate single predictor of upward social and economic mobility in America, more important than family background, education, race, intelligence, connections, or virtually any other single factor. To keep moving forward, think of the future, but act today.

✳   ✳   ✳

It's important to remember that all leaders face challenges, no matter how high or low their station in life. For example, former CEO of General Electric Jeff

Immelt said this after the September 11 attacks: "My second day as chairman, a plane that I lease, flying with engines I built, crashed into a building that I insure, and it was covered with a network I own." That's what you call a tough day for a leader.

Your challenges may not be as difficult or tragic as Immelt's. But every leader faces the strategy challenge at one time or another. With open eyes, the right mind-set, a willingness to take risks, a strategy, and a good team, you can rise to the occasion. And you can win.

6

The Communication Challenge

Getting Everyone on the Same Page

When most leaders think about communication, they focus on vision casting and giving direction. But communication is so much more than that—especially during tough times. Many people in the workplace today feel dehumanized and demoralized. They believe that the leaders and organizations they work for don't care about them as people. This can be particularly true when the future is uncertain.

To counter that, engage with people. Connect with them. Ask questions. Really listen. Make communication a conversation, not a monologue. Not only will you lift the morale of your team, you will get the best from them, and you will enjoy working *together* to find success.

Listen to Understand

I believe most leaders are naturally better at talking than listening. I know that was true for me when I was early in my leadership journey. I was intent on communicating my vision to others and making sure they understood my agenda. I wanted communication to go only one way—from me to them. The result was that few people bought into my leadership or my vision. I failed to realize that the road to vision buy-in was a two-way communication. That meant I had to learn how to listen. And with the goal of understanding.

Too often, as leaders, we get fixated on our own point of view and spend our time trying to convince others of our opinions instead of trying to find out their perspectives. We often make faulty assumptions about other people:

- We believe people are good at the same things we are good at—they aren't.
- We believe people are energized by the same things that energize us—they aren't.

- We believe people see the big picture in the same way we do—they don't.

Leaders who listen to understand are able to gather information, challenge assumptions, and modify their approach to their people. All of this enables them to lead more effectively. More than that, listening with no agenda speaks volumes to team members:

Listening to Understand Demonstrates That You Value People

Author and professor David W. Augsburger says, "Being heard is so close to being loved that for the average person they are almost indistinguishable." Because that is true, when you listen to others, you communicate that you care about them and value them.

Listening to Understand Has High Influence Value

One of the best ways to persuade others is with your ears. That may seem counterintuitive, because we expect persuasion to involve speaking. But when a leader listens to members of the team, that act gives the leader greater credibility and therefore influence. In contrast, when team members no longer believe that

their leader listens to understand them, they start looking around for someone who will.

Listening to Understand Leads to Learning

Sometimes people need to talk through a problem to
define it to themselves. When you simply listen as they
share their thoughts, without offering your own opinions, it can empower them to keep processing. And they
might come up with the best solution without a word
from you. Nothing is more satisfying to me as a leader
than to watch my team find answers not through my
words but through my ears. One of the greatest gifts I
can give a person is the gift of attention.

How Good Are Your Listening Skills?

I have to confess that I have not always been a good
listener. I talked too much and listened too little. I had
a quick solution for every problem and was all too
eager to share it. But that attitude hurt me. I damaged
some relationships because I didn't listen. And I often
failed to benefit from the advice and ideas of those
around me.

I've improved in this area, but I still have to guard
against talking too much and not listening enough. If

you also need to do that, you may benefit from this list of questions that I developed to help myself to keep listening:

1. Do I Have an Open-Ear Policy?

High Point University president Nido Qubein believes "most of us tend to suffer from 'agenda anxiety,' the feeling that what we want to say to others is more important than what we think they might want to say to us." Do you find that to be true? I do. I must admit it has taken me years to soften my natural inclination to direct others. How do I do that? As a leader I work to listen first, then lead.

2. Do I Interrupt?

Interrupting is impolite and is a symptom of an attitude problem. People with strong opinions or clear vision can have a tendency to cut to the chase, interrupt, and discount what others have to say. The problem is that interrupting translates to "What I want to say is more important than what you are saying."

3. Do I Want to Hear What I Need to Hear?

Effective leaders encourage others to tell them what they need to hear, even when it's not what they want to hear. Max De Pree said, "The first responsibility of a leader is to define reality." That can happen only when the leader is willing to hear and face the truth.

Create an Environment Where Questions Are Welcome

A wise leader once told me, "Before you attempt to *set* things right, make sure you *see* things right." That advice helped me to understand that most miscommunication is a result of people's having different assumptions. We can correct those wrong assumptions and prevent miscommunication by asking questions.

Creating an environment where people are willing to ask and answer questions leads to high morale and positive results. Here's how you can do that:

- **Value each team member:** When leaders ask questions and really listen to each answer, they show that they value the individuals on the team. Sam Walton said, "Asking and hearing people's opinions has a greater effect on them than telling them, 'Good job.'"
- **Value questions more than answers:** Questions lead to thinking and discussion. The process is often more valuable than the answer.

- **Value the potential of your team:** When I sit with my team, the first thing I do is eliminate positional authority and divisions. I value contribution much more than title or tenure.
- **Value the improvement of a good idea:** Great ideas are a result of several good ones put together. Let everyone at the table know that the best idea will be the one you all will embrace.

Author C. S. Lewis said, "The next best thing to being wise oneself is to live in a circle of those who are." You can do that by creating a positive environment for questions.

Ask the Right Questions

Listening is important for leaders, but if they don't ask the right questions, they're missing a lot. I ask questions of my team continually. It has become a constant in my leadership that I do almost automatically both one-on-one and within groups. And my team has been shaped by those questions. I worked with key members of my own team—Linda Eggers, Charlie Wetzel, Stephanie Wetzel, Mark Cole, David Hoyt, and my wife Margaret—to identify the questions I ask my team all the time. The questions below are not listed in order of importance, but each question is important, because they have defined our team.

"What Do You Think?"

These words come out of my mouth a dozen or more times every day. There are several benefits to asking people what they think at different times, including...

Gathering Information

I believe leaders see more than others see and see things before others do. But obviously leaders don't see *everything*. Asking people what they think helps you gather additional information that gives you a better idea of what's going on.

Confirming Your Intuition

We are all intuitive in our areas of strength. If you think you know something, but you're not sure why, ask someone you trust and respect. Their answers can often put words to your feelings and confirm your intuition, giving you greater certainty as you plan or make decisions.

Assessing Someone's Judgment or Leadership

When new people join your team, ask what they think. It helps you learn if they read the room right.

This is the fastest way to assess people's thinking and observation abilities.

One of your jobs as a leader is to piece all these bits of information together into a complete picture so you can make good decisions.

"What Do You Need?"

If you are not asking the members of your team how you can serve them, you may be holding them up. To find out, go to each team member individually and ask, "What could I do for you that would make your job easier, make you more successful, and make the team better?" Listen without interrupting to what people have to say, and then try to figure out ways to do what you can to serve them.

When You Speak, Be Honest and Helpful

Now we'll move on to the aspect that defines communication for most people: speaking. But now you know that it should come after listening and asking questions. When it's time to speak, you need to make it your goal to lift up team members and help them do their best. The leader sets the tone more than anyone else on a team, in a department, or for an organization. Their attitude is contagious. If they are positive, encouraging, and open to different ideas, so are their people. If you want your words to connect and yield results, recognize their influence and use it to benefit everyone.

Lifting others up does not mean focusing only on the positive. Just because you care about people doesn't mean you avoid correcting their work. If you care about people, treat them with respect, and build positive relationships with them, you actually have increased opportunities to have hard conversations with them that will help them to grow and perform better.

Every person has problems and makes mistakes in the workplace. This can be particularly true when you're working in tough times. As a leader, you have the responsibility and the privilege to be the person who helps them get through and get better. If you want to help people as a leader, you need to be willing to have tough conversations.

Balance Care with Candor

The most effective leaders are skilled at being relational while still helping people move forward. Care and candor must be in balance. Care without candor creates dysfunctional relationships. Candor without care creates distant relationships. But care balanced with candor creates developing relationships. This is how care

and candor work together to help you encourage results
and growth through communication:

Caring *Values the Person While* Candor *Values the Person's Potential*

Caring for others demonstrates that you value them,
and that is the foundation of a solid relationship. However,
if you want to help people get better, you have to be honest
about where they need to improve. That shows that you
value the person's potential. And that requires candor.

One of the secrets of being candid is to think, speak,
and act in terms of who the person has the potential to
become and to think about how you can help them to
reach it. If you're candid with others but with their benefit in mind, it can be similar to the work of a surgeon.
It may hurt, but it is meant to help and it shouldn't harm.

Caring *Establishes the Relationship While* Candor *Expands the Relationship*

Common ground and care help to establish a relationship. But to expand a relationship, candor and open
communication are required. Most leaders I talk to
have a difficult conversation that they know they need
to have but are avoiding. Usually they are reluctant for
one of two reasons: Either they don't like confrontation,
or they fear that they will hurt the person they need to

talk to. But if a leader can balance care and candor, it will actually deepen and strengthen the relationship.

Not everyone responds well to candid conversations. Let's face it: Honesty can hurt. Some people shut down when you criticize them. Others leave and work somewhere else. However, if you have candid conversations, you give them an opportunity to improve, and they often hang in there and grow.

Caring *Defines the Relationship While* Candor *Directs the Relationship*

Just because people care about one another doesn't mean that they are going anywhere together. Getting the team moving together to accomplish a goal is the responsibility of the leader, and that often requires candor.

Retired army general and former secretary of state Colin Powell noted, "Good leadership involves responsibility to the welfare of the group, which means that some people will get angry at your actions and decisions. It's inevitable—if you're honorable." If you want to lead people well, you need to be willing to direct them candidly.

The bottom line, which has already become very clear, is that good leaders must embrace both care and candor. You can't ignore either. So to help you keep the balance between the two, I've created a caring candor checklist for working with people. Before having a candid conversation, make sure that you can answer yes to the following questions:

- Have I invested enough in the relationship to be candid with this person?
- Do I truly value this person as a person?
- Am I sure this is this person's issue and not mine?
- Am I sure I'm not speaking up because I feel threatened?
- Is the issue more important than the relationship?
- Does this conversation clearly serve this person's interests and not just mine?
- Am I willing to invest time and energy to help this person change?
- Am I willing to show this person how to do something, not just say what's wrong?
- Am I willing and able to set clear, specific expectations?

If you can answer yes to all of these questions, then your motives are probably right and you have a good chance of being able to communicate effectively.

Candid conversations are a leader's responsibility and must be done—but in the right way with the right attitude. When an employee is hired to get a certain job done and doesn't, that hurts the team and the organization. And then it's time for the leader to take action. That can be very hard, but in the long term, it's best not only for the organization but also for the person who needs to hear what's not going right.

The next time you find yourself in a place where you need to have a candid conversation, just remember this:

- Do it quickly—shovel the pile while it's small.
- Do it calmly, never in anger—use the caring candor checklist.
- Do it privately—you want to help the person, not embarrass him or her.
- Do it thoughtfully, in a way that minimizes embarrassment or intimidation.

If your goal is to help the individual, improve the team, and fulfill the vision of the organization, then this is the path you should follow as a leader.

As you work with people and have candid conversations, allow me to remind you of one more thing: Candidness is a two-way street. If you want to be an effective leader, you must allow the people you work with to be candid with you. You must solicit feedback. And you must be mature and secure enough to take in people's criticism without defensiveness and learn from it.

If you care about your people, you'll want to be honest with them in a way that helps them. When you see that someone on your team is making mistakes or in some way falling short, plan to talk with the person immediately. Use the caring candor checklist to make sure you do it in the right way. And remember, it's hard to go wrong as long as you're practicing the Golden Rule.

Do Whatever It Takes to Make the Complex Clear

Effective leaders never assume that their team members understand their message. They don't take anything for granted. This is never more important than when navigating tough times. Don't assume your team knows what you know or believes what you believe. Don't assume they all understand how their talents and efforts are supposed to contribute to the mission of the team. Fuzzy communication leads to unclear direction, which produces sloppy execution. Successful leaders create an uncomplicated link between the vision of the organization and everyday production of the team. They explain in clear terms how the short term impacts the long term.

By being clear in their communication, they continually point the way for their team.

Start with a Clear and Compelling Vision

The vision you communicate should be simple and well-defined, yet expansive and challenging. It is aligned with the shared values of the team. It is focused primarily on the end, not necessarily the details of the means. It matches the giftedness of the team. And when it is understood, it fills the room with energy! To effectively communicate the vision, make sure it does the following simply and clearly. A vision that motivates the team to action...

Defines Success

In every organization I have led, I found it necessary to define or redefine what success meant for the people working there. How in the world can an organization be successful if the people in it don't know what the target is?

Describes Each Person's Part in Achieving Success

A sports team can't win unless each player is very clear on their role in achieving a higher score than the opposing team at the end of the game. Effective leaders explain, demonstrate, and reiterate exactly how each team member will help achieve the win. They also offer corrections (balancing care and candor) whenever people make mistakes or don't work hard enough to fulfill their role. When team members are clear on their tasks, and on how those tasks relate to the goal, they have the tools to do their work with excellence and help everyone win.

Shares How Success Will Be Measured and Celebrated

If you want your people to be inspired to win, then communicate how their efforts will be measured and how victories—small and large—will be celebrated. Then make sure to follow through on those celebrations. And share your own personal victories with them whenever possible, giving them as much of the credit as you can. That not only motivates people, but also helps them to enjoy the journey.

Good leaders communicate the vision of the organization once, then continually remind the team of it. They don't stop there. They also communicate the vision through their own actions. Modeling the vision helps people understand and embrace it in ways they may not have before. When followers witness the leader's positive results and see goals being met, they get a clearer picture of what it means to fulfill the vision.

Effective leaders continually strive to help their people understand and embrace the vision for a win. They share and refine how each team member contributes to that vision. And they point out and celebrate every victory. That encourages members of the team. It validates their efforts. It makes the vision that much clearer. Each victory also expands the vision, because with increased confidence and skill, the people doing the work recognize that they can actually accomplish more than they may have believed was possible.

* * *

During tough times, communication may be the leader's most important skill. Everything else hinges on it. You can't be a change agent if you can't communicate why and how the change needs to happen. You can't strategize collaboratively if you don't know how to listen and ask questions effectively. Great communication opens doors and hearts. It increases your team's trust in you and their belief that you want to help them. The best communication inspires and compels people to strive for a win, because they own the process and know success will benefit everyone.

7

The Decision-Making Challenge

Keeping Everyone on the New Course

The greatest challenge in leadership is making decisions that affect other people, and in tough times you may face more of those kinds of decisions. It's hard to make decisions every day on behalf of others and be confident that they will have positive results. Some leaders would rather act like the French revolutionary who said, "There go my people. I must find out where they're going, so I can lead them."

Decision making for the team can be difficult and painful. But to lead through tough times, you must be willing to make them. That's because as you implement your strategies and lead your team, conditions will continue to change. Some things you try won't work. Some team members will make mistakes. You will discover additional problems. All of these conditions require new decisions. If you use your head, include your team, and do what you believe is best for your people and the organization, your odds of keeping on course and making it through the challenges greatly increase.

The Kinds of Decisions You Will Face

As you lead your team in pursuit of a win, new challenges will arise. Here are some of the decisions you will encounter:

Courageous Decisions: What Must Be Done

Hard-won progress often comes as the result of difficult decisions that can be scary. Sometimes the organization is on the line and the only people in a position to make the courageous calls are the leaders.

Priority Decisions: What Must Be Done First

It is the responsibility of leaders to look ahead, see the bigger picture, understand the greater vision, and make decisions based on the priorities of the whole team and organization.

Change Decisions: What Must Be Done Differently

One of the most difficult yet vital roles of leaders is to be change agents for the sake of the team and organization. Most people don't like change. They fear it and resist it. Leaders often provide the education and impetus for making changes.

Creative Decisions: What Might Be Possible

Sometimes making tough decisions calls for experience. But often what's really beneficial is creativity. Good leaders think outside the box and help the team break through barriers and cover new ground.

People Decisions: Who Should—and Should Not—Be Involved

It's not always easy to find the right person for a given job. It's even more difficult to decide whether someone is no longer right for the team.

Though decision making is difficult, it is vital to good leadership. H. W. Andrews asserted, "Failure to make a decision after due consideration of all the facts will quickly brand a man as unfit for a position of responsibility. Not all of your decisions will be correct. None of us is perfect. But if you get into the habit of making decisions, experience will develop your judgment to a point where more and more of your decisions will be right." And as a result, you will become a better leader.

Resist the Pressure to Veer Off Course

In our fast-paced and complicated culture, I think just about everyone feels some kind of pressure, and that pressure is compounded during difficult times. And with pressure comes temptation. You might be pushed to cut corners or bend the truth. Corporate executives can feel pressure to increase stock value at all costs. Salespeople feel pressure to make more sales. Students feel pressure to get higher grades. No one escapes pressure. So the question is how are you going to deal with it?

Expect and Prepare for These Pressures

Since leadership pressures are inevitable, it would be wise to know and prepare for your enemy. Pressure will tempt you to compromise, which can put your success in jeopardy. Here are some pressures you might face, and how they might make you lose:

- **The Pressure to Make Rash Emotional Decisions.** Pressure ratchets up emotion, and strong emotions can make thinking foggy. But good thinking is what's needed before any decision. The only way to gain clarity of thinking in emotional situations is to pause. Decisions made at the height of emotion are often shortsighted and designed to reduce pressure, not necessarily solve the problem. Their impact is usually negative. Too many rash decisions, and your progress can halt, veer off course, or even go backward.

- **The Pressure to Deny the Truth.** Mistakes will happen in your team's pursuit of a win. But some people find it almost impossible to admit making one. If you or team members deny the truth, you will end up trying to make a decision without all the data. What is the likelihood of making a good decision in that scenario?

- **The Pressure to Take Shortcuts.** Someone once said that the longest distance between two points is a shortcut. While that may be true, pressure often points out what looks like an easier path off the road that will bypass a difficult challenge. It's easy to believe that's true. Here is how to spot a shortcut: They tend to look easier in the short run. But they risk a huge cost in the long run.

- **The Pressure to Abandon Commitments.** Molière said, "Men are alike in their promises.

It is only in their deeds that they differ." Pressure can make following through on commitments look impossible. Then it tempts you to stop looking for ways to keep your word. But the price of breaking promises is high. And a good solution to your problem can usually be found if you search beyond what looks impossible.

- **The Pressure to Bow to Others' Opinions.** Pressure often comes out of the mouths of other people. Sometimes, even disguised as good advice from people you trust. It's important to weigh the opinions, fears, or even pleas of others against what you know to be your mission. If you have a tendency to give in to the needs or opinions of others, you must fight to do what's right, even when it's unpopular.

- **The Pressure to Make Promises You Can't or Don't Intend to Keep.** For some leaders, the pressure from other people can feel so great that they are tempted to simply say what those others want to hear. But those words have power to destroy trust when they do not become reality. Samuel Johnson said, "They ought not to raise expectations which it is not in our power to satisfy, and that it is more pleasing to see smoke brightening into flame, than flame sinking into smoke." It's crucial for leaders to avoid making promises that are likely to go up in smoke.

Remember What's at Stake

In order to make decisions that benefit the team and your long-term goals, leaders must always keep in mind what is at stake. And during tough times, the stakes are usually high. They don't just include the team's ability to weather the crisis or remain on the path toward victory. Your leadership credibility is also at stake. That includes trust in your positive motives, your competence, and your integrity.

Your Integrity:
It Rises and Falls Based on the Code
You Live By

Another name for a code of behavior is ethics. And I should point out here that I believe there's no such thing as business ethics or leadership ethics or the ethics that apply during tough times—there's only ethics. Think about it. When people compartmentalize, using one set of ethics for their professional life, another for their spiritual life, and still another at home with their family, they build a house of cards. And it will eventually come crashing down.

Ethics is ethics. And there are really only two important considerations in being ethical. The first is a standard to follow. The second is the will to follow it.

A Standard to Follow

In today's current relativistic culture—where everyone wants to use different standards and where every situation is supposed to require its own code of conduct—I find it promising that people from every culture still seem to agree on one standard: the Golden Rule. And while that term and its definition arise in our culture from Christianity, I learned from one of my mentors, Fred Smith, that a golden rule exists in just about every culture and belief system. Here are some of the variations:

Christianity: "Do to others whatever you would like them to do to you."[7]

Islam: "None of you has faith until he loves for his brother or his neighbor what he loves for himself."[8]

Judaism: "What is hateful to you, do not do to your fellow man. This is the entire Law; all the rest is commentary."[9]

Buddhism: "Hurt not others in ways that you yourself would find hurtful."[10]

Hinduism: "This is the sum of duty; do naught unto others what you would not have them do unto you."[11]

Zoroastrianism: "Whatever is disagreeable to yourself do not do unto others."[12]

Confucianism: "Do not do unto others what you would not have them do to you."[13]

Bahai: "And if thine eyes be turned towards justice, choose thou for thy neighbour that which thou choosest for thyself."[14]

Jainism: "A man should wander about treating all creatures as he himself would be treated."[15]

Yoruba Proverb (Nigeria): "One going to take a pointed stick to pinch a baby bird should first try it on himself to feel how it hurts."[16]

This concept of treating people the way you would want to be treated is embraced by people from nearly every part of the world. It's the closest thing to a universal guideline for ethics that we can find. When described to people who are not spiritual or religious, they usually acknowledge its truth as well. After all, who wants to be treated worse than they treat others?

One of our problems is that ethics is never a business issue or a social issue or a political issue. It is always a personal issue. People say they want integrity. But at the same time, ironically, studies indicate that the majority of people don't always act with the kind of integrity they request from others. The same person who cheats on his taxes or steals office supplies wants honesty and integrity from the corporation whose stock he buys, the politician he votes for, and the client he deals with in his own business.

It's easy to *discuss* ethics and even easier to be *disgusted* with people who fail the ethics test—especially when we have been violated by the wrongdoing of others. It's harder to make ethical choices in our own lives. In the 1980s, former president Ronald Reagan quipped that when it comes to the economy, it's a recession when your neighbor loses his job, but it's a depression when you lose yours! Ethics is similar. It's always harder when I'm the one having to make the choice.

I want to be ethical, and I believe that you do too. Furthermore, I know it really is possible to do what's right *and* succeed in business.

The Will to Follow It

When it comes to ethics, it's usually easy to make the big decisions. Most people don't have a tough time deciding *not* to commit murder. Few people are tempted to steal a car or break into someone's house. However, the little things can be harder to manage. But to be accounted trustworthy, a person must be predictable. When you manage your life and all the little decisions by the Golden Rule, you create an ethical predictability in your life. People will have confidence in you, knowing that you consistently do the right thing.

As you apply the Golden Rule to your life and make decisions according to it, remember this:

- **Decisions, Not Conditions, Determine Your Ethics:** People of poor character tend to blame their choices on circumstances. Ethical people make good choices regardless of circumstances. If they make enough good choices, they begin to *create* better conditions for themselves.

- **Wrong Decisions Leave Scars:** Every time people make wrong decisions, there is an impact, even if they don't immediately notice it.

- **The More People Involved, the Greater the Pressure for Conformity:** Ethical decisions made in private have their own pressure, because one may be tempted to believe that a private indiscretion will never become public knowledge. Public decisions involving other people carry a different kind of pressure—that of conformity. No matter how much pressure there is, you can't allow others to force you into making unethical decisions.

- **Inaction Is Also a Decision:** Some people's reaction to ethical decision making is to avoid taking action. However, it's important to remember that inaction is also a decision. There are thousands of people who choose every day not to act when they see their employers cut corners or compromise ethics—and who ultimately will live with the consequences.

To live an ethical life, you must hold to your principles as you make tough decisions. Edward R. Lyman stated, "Principle—particularly moral principle—can never be a weather vane, spinning around this way and that with the shifting winds of expediency. Moral principle is a compass forever fixed and forever true—and that is as important in business as it is in the classroom."

Why Leaders Crack Under Pressure

I believe when people make unethical choices, they do so for one of three reasons:

1. They Do What's Most Convenient

An ethical dilemma can be defined as an undesirable or unpleasant choice relating to a moral principle or practice. What do we do in such situations? Do we do the easy thing or the right thing? As human beings, we seem prone to failing personal ethics tests. We do something even when we know it's wrong because it's easier. We cheat because we think we won't get caught. We give ourselves permission to cut corners because we rationalize that it's just one time. It's our way of dealing with pressure.

2. They Do What They Must to Win

I think most people are like me: I hate losing! Businesspeople in particular desire to win through achievement and success. But many think they have to choose between being ethical and winning. Many people believe that embracing ethics would limit their options, their opportunities, their very ability to succeed in business. They agree with Harvard history professor Henry Adams, who stated, "Morality is a private and costly luxury." If you believe you have only two choices— (1) to win by doing whatever it takes, even if it's unethical; or (2) to have ethics and lose—you're faced with a real moral dilemma. Few people set out with the desire to be dishonest, but nobody wants to lose.

3. They Rationalize Their Choices with Relativism

Many people choose to deal with no-win situations by deciding what's right in the moment, according to their circumstances. The result is ethical chaos. Everyone has his own standards, which change from situation to situation. Making matters worse is people's natural inclination to be easy on themselves, judging themselves according to their *good intentions*—while holding others to a higher standard and judging them by their *worst actions*. Where once our decisions were based on ethics, now ethics are based on our decisions. If it's good for me, then it's good. Where is this trend likely to end?

If you embrace ethical behavior, will it automatically make you rich and successful? Of course not. Can it pave the way for you to become successful? Absolutely! *Ethics + Competence* is a winning equation. In contrast, people who continually attempt to test the edge of ethics inevitably go over that edge. Shortcuts never pay off in the long run. It may be possible to fool people for a season, but in the long haul, their deeds will catch up with them because the truth does come out. In the short term, behaving ethically may look like a loss (just as one can temporarily appear to win by being unethical). However, in the long term, people always lose when they live without ethics. Have you ever met anyone who lived a life of shortcuts, deception, and cheating who finished well?

Remember Whom to Include

Many leaders believe that they need to have all the answers. After all, if they admit that they don't know something, it shows weakness. And if they show weakness, how are they going to stay on top of the hill? Successful leaders think differently.

A leader's job is not to know everything but to attract people who know things that he or she does not. One of us is not as smart as all of us. If you've tried to have all the answers, you need to make a change. Stop bringing people together to give them the answers and start calling on them to help you find the answers. It will transform your leadership, not only because you can be yourself and stop pretending that you know more than you do, but also because it harnesses the power of shared thinking.

Sometimes you'll need a number of different perspectives in order to discover the best one. That has been true for me and for members of my team. Sometimes they have needed to move me along and convince me of a decision they believe in. Sometimes it's the other way around, and I need to allow them time to come around. The give-and-take is very healthy.

If I push for something my team doesn't agree with, I do so because I'm sensing an opportunity or because my leadership intuition about it is strong. That doesn't mean I run over my team or force the issue. It usually means that I give them time to process and that I revisit the issue multiple times so they can continue to receive additional information.

In contrast, there are times when I step back and defer to members of my inner circle. If a person is closer to the issue than I am, and he or she has a track record of success, I defer. Decisions should always be made as close to the problem as possible. If the team member is going to be responsible for carrying the endeavor forward, I am more likely to defer. And if team members keep coming back with an idea or decision and do so with great passion, I am likely to reconsider my stance or decision and defer to them.

More than once, members of my team have saved me from making a bad or stupid decision because they saw things I didn't see, relied on experience I didn't have, or shared wisdom they possessed that I lacked. Their thinking has elevated my ability, and for that I am very grateful.

Good leaders *never* take people out of the equation in anything they do. They always take people into account—where they are, what they believe, what they're feeling. Every question they ask is expressed in the context of people. Knowing what to do isn't enough to make someone a good leader. Just because something is right doesn't necessarily mean that people will let you do it. Good leaders take that into account. And they think and plan accordingly.

If you want to be successful as a leader, you must think less in terms of systems and more in terms of people's emotions. You must think more in terms of human capacity and less in terms of regulations. You must think more in terms of buy-in and less in terms of procedures. In other words, you must think of people before you try to achieve progress.

Build a Strong Decision-Making Foundation

I've already talked about the danger of making decisions at the height of emotion. But it's also crucial to not make decisions at an emotional low point. When you're in an emotional valley, your perspective isn't good. Everything looks difficult. The mountains around you look huge. In contrast, when you're on the mountaintop, you can see almost everything. So whenever possible, try to make major decisions when you have good perspective. Aside from pausing until you can think rationally, make sure to also:

1. Do Your Homework

The first defense against having unfiltered emotions negatively affect your decision making is to consider the facts. Define the issue. Put it in writing if needed. Then gather information, considering the credibility of your sources. The more solid information you have, the better you can fight irrational emotions.

2. List Your Options and Where They Could Lead

Another part of the fact-finding process is to think about outcomes. Brainstorm every option you can think of and what the potential results could be. This will help you root out ideas that feel good emotionally but aren't strong rationally.

3. Seek Advice from the Right People

There are two kinds of people you need to consult. The first group includes the people necessary to make a decision happen. If they aren't on board, you will be in trouble if you make the decision. The second consists of people with success in the area of consideration who have your interests at heart. They can give you good advice.

4. Listen to Your Instincts

You don't want your emotions to run away with you when you're making decisions, but you also don't want to ignore your instincts. Often your instincts warn you in a way that goes beyond the facts. Psychologist Joyce

Brothers advised, "Trust your hunches...Hunches are usually based on facts filed away just below the conscious level."

When all is said and done, you must be able to live with the decisions you make. When I have to make a difficult or emotional decision, I am inspired by Abraham Lincoln, who said, "I desire to so conduct the affairs of this Administration that if, at the end, when I come to lay down the reins of power, I have lost every other friend on earth, I shall at least have one friend left, and that friend shall be down inside of me."

✶   ✶   ✶

Whenever you see an organization during a challenging season, you can be sure that its leaders have made some very tough decisions—and are continuing to make them. Success is an uphill journey. People don't coast their way to effective leadership. As billionaire oilman and environmental advocate T. Boone Pickens says, "Be willing to make decisions. That's the most important quality in a good leader."

Conclusion

One of the principles of leadership that I think is particularly important in difficult times was articulated by John W. Gardner, former secretary of health, education, and welfare. He said, "The first and last task of a leader is to keep hope alive—the hope that we can finally find our way through to a better world—despite the day's action, despite our own inertness and shallowness and wavering resolve." Hope is the foundation of change. If we continue to hold hope high, and we help others to do the same, there is always a chance to move forward and succeed.

Crisis offers the opportunity to be reborn. Difficult times can discipline us to become stronger. Conflict can actually renew our chances of building better relationships. It's not always easy to remember these things.

But as leaders, we must remind people of the possibilities and to help them succeed. As I've often said, everything rises and falls on leadership. If you have been trusted to lead, you have an opportunity to raise people up through tough times. I hope you will embrace that challenge.

Notes

1. Hal Urban, *Life's Greatest Lessons: 20 Things That Matter* (New York: Fireside, 2003), 12.

2. James Casey, "Climb the Steep," PoemHunter.com, http://www.poemhunter.com/poem/climb-the-steep/, accessed September 25, 2012.

3. Warren W. Wiersbe, *In Praise of Plodders!* (Grand Rapids, MI: Kregel, 1991).

4. Stephen R. Covey, *Principle-Centered Leadership* (New York: Fireside, 1992), 246.

5. Wolf J. Rinke, *Winning Management: Six Fail-Safe Strategies for Building High-Performance Organizations* (Clarksville, MD: Achievement Publishers, 1997), 212.

6. Robert H. Schuller, *Tough Times Never Last, but Tough People Do!* (New York: Bantam Books, 1984), 73.

7. Matthew 7:12, NLT.

8. *Sahih Muslim*, book 1, number 72, quoted in "Golden Rule in Islam," Islam.ru, February 26, 2013.

9. *Talmud*, Shabbat 3id, quoted in "The Universality of the Golden Rule in World Religions," http://www.teachingvalues.com/goldenrule.html.

10. Udana-Varga 5, 1, quoted in "The Universality of the Golden Rule in World Religions."

11. Mahabharata 5, 1517, quoted in "The Universality of the Golden Rule in World Religions."

12. Shayast-na-Shayast 13:29, quoted in "The Golden Rule Is Universal," Golden Rule Project, https://www.goldenruleproject.org/formulations.

13. Analects 15:23, quoted in "The Golden Rule Is Universal."

14. Epistle to the Son of the Wolf, quoted in "The Golden Rule Is Universal."

15. Sutrakritanga 1.11.33, quoted in "The Golden Rule Is Universal."

16. African proverb quoted in "The Golden Rule Is Universal."

About the Author

JOHN C. MAXWELL is a #1 *New York Times* bestselling author, speaker, coach, and leader who has sold more than 33 million books in fifty languages. He has been called the #1 leader in business and the most influential leadership expert in the world. His organizations—the John Maxwell Company, the John Maxwell Team, EQUIP, and the John Maxwell Leadership Foundation—have translated his teachings into seventy languages and used them to train millions of leaders from every country in the world. A recipient of the Horatio Alger Award and the Mother Teresa Prize for Global Peace and Leadership from the Luminary Leadership Network, Dr. Maxwell influences *Fortune* 500 CEOs, the presidents of nations, and entrepreneurs worldwide. For more information about him visit JohnMaxwell.com.